Sunset

ORCHIDS

BY JOHN R. DUNMIRE AND THE EDITORS OF SUNSET BOOKS

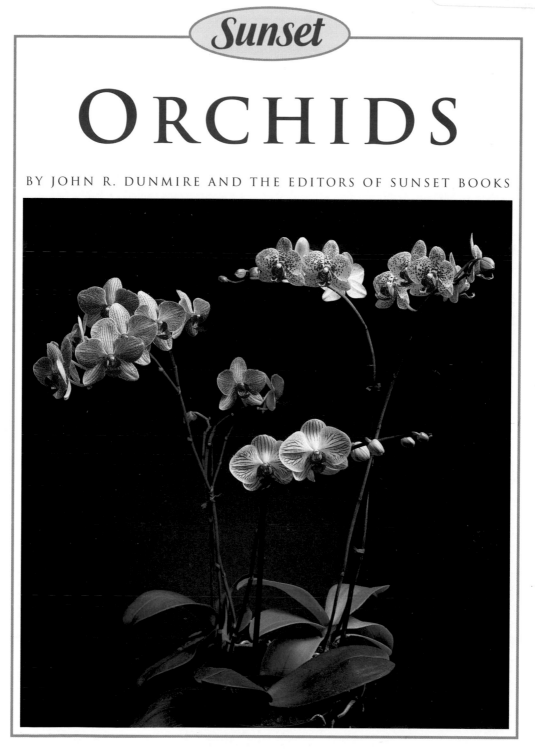

SUNSET BOOKS • MENLO PARK, CALIFORNIA

THE WORLD OF ORCHIDS REVEALED

Exotic, fascinating, beautiful, mysterious . . . adjectives seem inexhaustible in describing the orchid family—as, too, do the variety and number of species that you can grow. As you'll soon discover through the pages of this book, the world of orchids is one that a beginning grower can easily enter, but also one that never seems to show its limits to the experienced grower.

For many years the two previous editions of the Sunset book *Orchids* have guided gardeners through the intricacies of growing these endlessly fascinating plants. Still, since the last edition was published new orchids have been discovered and brought into cultivation, countless new hybrids created, and new knowledge and experience disseminated. We have therefore distilled this new information into the expanded edition that you hold in your hands.

A wide world of orchids awaits you beyond the narrow range of varieties that are commonly sold. We hope that the information and stunning photographs contained in this book will tempt you to explore it.

We wish to thank the following consultants and nurseries for their valuable advice and assistance: Baker & Chantry Orchids, Woodinville, Washington; Michael Glikbarg, Orchids of Los Osos, Los Osos, California; Paul Gripp, Santa Barbara Orchid Estate, Santa Barbara, California; Cordelia Head, J & L Orchids, Easton, Connecticut; Heronswood Nursery, Kingston, Washington; Marianne R. Matthews, orchid breeder, Accredited Judge, American Orchid Society, Houston, Texas; Ned Nash, American Orchid Society, West Palm Beach, Florida; Marvel Sherrill and Larry Wright, Jr., Ph.D., The Rod McLellan Company, South San Francisco, California.

SUNSET BOOKS

VP, General Manager, Richard A. Smeby
VP, Editorial Director, Bob Doyle
Production Director: Lory Day
Art Director: Vaskin Guiragossian

Staff for this book
Managing Editor: Marianne Lipanovich
Sunset Books Senior Editor, Gardening: Suzanne Normand Eyre
Copy Editor and Indexer: Pamela Evans
Photo Researcher: Tishana Peebles
Production Coordinator: Patricia S. Williams
Proofreader: Claudia A. Blaine

Art Director: Alice Rogers
Page Layouts: Elisa Tanaka
Illustrator: Sarah A. Young
Computer Production: Fog Press

Cover: *Zygopetalum*. Photography by Norman A. Plate.
Border photograph (cymbidiums) by William B. Dewey.

5 6 7 8 9 0   QPD/QPD   9 8 7 6 5 4 3 2 1

PHOTOGRAPHERS:

Greg Allikas: 2, 7, 12 top, 19 bottom, 21 top, 25 top, center right, and bottom, 26 top, 32 bottom right, 33 bottom, 34, 36, 37, 45 top, 52, 56, 57, 60 bottom right, 61 top, 62 top, 63 center, 69 top, 70, 71 top, 72 bottom, 75, 78 top, 84, 85 left, 94 bottom, 100, 111 bottom; **Richard Clark:** 11 bottom, 12 bottom, 58, 59 top, 61 center, 62 bottom left and right, 63 bottom, 68 top right, 76 top, 78 bottom, 80 right, 86, 88 top, 89, 93 bottom, 94 top, 95 bottom, 98, 99 bottom, 110; **Claire Curran:** 79 right; **Alan and Linda Detrick:** 25 center left, 60 bottom left, 71 bottom, 76 bottom, 83, 90, 96 top, 99 top, 105; **William B. Dewey:** 28, 47 top; **Derek Fell:** 4, 12 center, 48 bottom, 51 bottom, 74 right, 92 bottom, 95 top, 101 top, back cover bottom left; **Lynne Harrison:** 16, 33 top, 45 bottom, 48 top, 49 right, 50, 51 top, 81 left and right, 97, 106 right; **John Humble:** 9, 38; **Kusra Kapuler:** 11 top, 44, 49 left, 60 center, 63 top, 69 bottom, 77 top, 91 top, 106 top left; **Ells Marugg:** 18, 21 bottom, 26 center left, center right, and bottom, 31, 46, 59 bottom, 60 top, 85 right, 102, 103 top, 106 bottom left, 111 top, back cover right; **courtesy of The Rod McLellan Co.:** 30, 55 bottom, 64, 82 top left, 92 top, 103 bottom, 104 left, back cover top left; **courtesy of Orchids of Los Osos:** 15, 66, 80 left, 82 bottom, 88 bottom; **Ron Parsons:** 59 center, 72 top, 77 bottom, 87 bottom left, 96 bottom, 101 bottom; **Pamela K. Peirce:** 32 top and bottom left, 79 left; **Norman A. Plate:** 14, 42, 47 bottom, 61 bottom, 65, 67, 108 left; **Charles Rowden:** 6, 19 top, 54, 68 top left and bottom, 71 center, 73, 74 left, 82 top right, 87 top left and right, 91 bottom, 93 top, 104 right, 107, 108 right, 109; **Richard Shiell:** 10; **Darrow M. Watt:** 1, 22, 24, 55 top.

CONTENTS

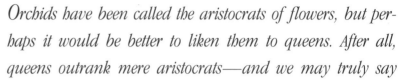

UNDERSTANDING ORCHIDS

Orchids have been called the aristocrats of flowers, but perhaps it would be better to liken them to queens. After all, queens outrank mere aristocrats—and we may truly say of the orchid, as Shakespeare did of Queen Cleopatra, that "age cannot wither her, nor custom stale her infinite variety." Once admired mainly in prom or opening-night corsages and as exotic displays in conservatories or botanical gardens, the orchid has now descended from her throne and is to be found in florist shops, nurseries, and even on the racks of discount stores and supermarkets. Orchid societies hold shows and sales in shopping malls, county fairgrounds, and many other venues, where it is possible to find a blooming plant for no more than you would pay for an azalea. Familiarity in this case, however, breeds not contempt but attempt, as new converts discover how surprisingly easy it is to grow orchids.

The most familiar orchids are phalaenopsis, cattleyas, cymbidiums, and paphiopedilums (lady's slipper orchids), but other kinds—notably dendrobiums, miltonias, and masdevallias—are gaining in popularity. In addition, there are countless others to lend variety to a collection.

The orchids spilling down the wall of this conservatory represent only a tiny fraction of the thousands of members of the orchid family.

A burst of color, called a splash pattern, is seen here on × *Laeliocattleya* 'Ontario' HCC/AOS. The colors of multihued orchids should be clear and well defined.

WHAT IS AN ORCHID?

The thousands of species of orchids make up an exceedingly varied family. Many orchids are so different in appearance that it's hard to believe they are related. Even given their amazing variety of sizes, shapes, and proportion of parts, orchids do have a number of mutual characteristics that distinguish them from other plants.

Botanically speaking, orchids are perennial plants with *zygomorphic*, or irregular, flowers (that is, they can be divided into two equal halves in only one plane—unlike, say, a rose or camellia flower, which can be divided in any of many planes). Flowers typically consist of three outer segments *(sepals)* and three inner segments *(petals)*, one of which is greatly modified in form and called the *labellum*, or lip.

The reproductive parts of the flower are concentrated in an organ known as the *column* (see the illustration below, left). The purpose of the many highly complex structures involving the lip and column is to ensure that the pollenizing agents (bees, flies, beetles, birds) will transfer pollen from one flower to another of the same species, preventing either self-pollination or cross-species pollination.

Many modifications of the flower structure occur: the lip may be enormously enlarged or reduced, the petals may be so reduced as to become nearly invisible, and

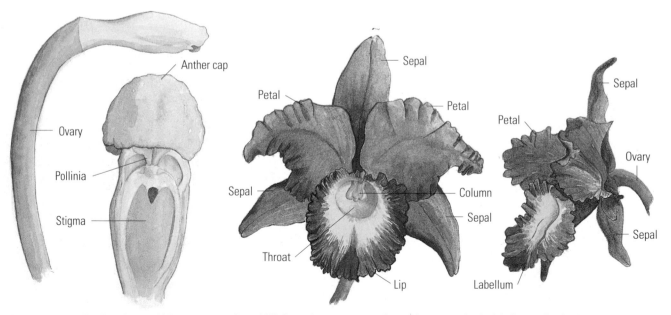

The column contains the stigma, which receives the pollen, and the anther cap, which holds it. Orchid pollen is clustered in compact masses called pollinia.

An orchid's flower has many parts: the petals, the sepals, the labellum or lip, the throat, and the column, which is sometimes hidden by the folds of lip. The ovary, or seed-bearing organ, is just below the flower and resembles a flower stalk.

A close-up look at a cattleya hybrid clearly shows the column and its parts.

Orchid flowers vary greatly. Above, a cattleya (TOP), masdevallia (CENTER), and paphiopedilum (BOTTOM) display their differences.

one or more of the floral parts may be fused or drawn out into long tails. These irregularities and the complex structure of the orchid flower give it a strange beauty—and, not surprisingly, other strangely beautiful flowers are often mistaken for orchids.

Orchid flowers come in all colors except true black (and *Coelogyne pandurata* has markings that approach true black), but the predominant colors are pink, lavender, red, yellow, and white. True blue is rare and much esteemed; brown and green are quite common, and many species have flowers marked with two or more contrasting colors. The highly fragrant zygopetalums commonly have green-and-brown sepals and petals, with a white lip marked in purple.

Flowers vary in size from nearly a foot across to mere pinheads. Many have fragrances ranging from fresh and fruity to sultry and exotic. (A few, it must be admitted, smell like carrion; these are not commonly grown!)

Orchids' growth habits are nearly as varied as their flowers. Many grow on trees (*epiphytes*) or rocks (*lithophytes*), surviving on rain and the nutrients brought them by decaying leaves and other organic detritus. None is a parasite; orchids may live on a tree, but they take no nourishment from it.

Others (*terrestrials*) live in the soil and may have fibrous roots, rhizomes, or tubers. A few (though not in cultivation) have no chlorophyll and live as *saprophytes* on decaying plant matter in the soil. Some familiar orchids are opportunists, sometimes living in pockets of leaf mold on rocks or in the crotches of trees, sometimes flourishing on the ground in rich, highly organic soil.

TWO TYPES OF GROWTH

Orchid plants increase their size in one of two ways. Those with *monopodial* growth (see the illustration below, left) become taller each year as a consequence of new growth forming only at the tip of the stem. Leaves are set in two rows on opposite sides of the stem, each one alternating with its partner. Flower spikes and aerial roots originate in a leaf joint or opposite a leaf. The stems may become tall, as in many species of *Vanda,* or may be so short as to be practically invisible, as in species of *Phalaenopsis.* Note that if these orchids' top growth becomes damaged, they may still produce new growth from dormant buds lower on the stem.

The second growth type, by far the more prevalent, is *sympodial* (see the illustration below, right). Here the upward growth of the plant stops, in most cases, after one season; the next year's growth arises from the base of the prior year's, extending the plant laterally (or vertically, if the plant is growing on a vertical surface). Sympodial orchids may bloom from the tips of the most recent growth, from its base, or from buds on older growths.

Many sympodial orchids develop thickened stems called *pseudobulbs;* these store water and food, enabling the plant to survive periods of drought. Pseudobulbs may be round and fat, flattened, or elongated into cylindrical stems usually called canes. They vary from microscopic to many feet in length. Leaves may grow either along the pseudobulbs or from their tips.

In monopodial growth, the central stem lengthens from a single point at the top of prior growth; aerial roots and flower stalks all originate from that same central stem. Vandas and phalaenopsis are good examples of monopodial growth.

Sympodial growth is typical of the majority of orchids. New growth arises from the base of the prior year's growth; it matures in one season, producing first flowers and then more new growth. Cattleyas and dendrobiums exemplify sympodial growth.

WHERE THEY GROW

A few terrestrial orchids grow north of the Arctic Circle, but many more grow in the temperate regions of Europe, Asia, and North America. A large number of terrestrials grow where the climate is "Mediterranean"—South Africa, the Mediterranean basin, Chile, and parts of Australia. Most of these tend to grow and bloom in winter and spring, resting during the dry months as tubers.

In cold-winter regions terrestrials overwinter as dormant tubers or rhizomes, and then grow, bloom, and set seed in spring and summer. In such areas of North America they are considered difficult to grow and are rarely seen as garden plants. However, a few species are available from mail-order sources, and their use is likely to grow slowly as more is learned about their cultural needs.

Epiphytic orchids are found chiefly in subtropical and tropical regions (although one, *Epidendrum conopseum*, grows as far north as North Carolina, and several Asiatic species range northward to Japan). Although often thought of as jungle plants, they are seldom found in dark, dank undergrowth. Most live on trees high above ground where light is plentiful, or on rocky ledges in clearings and at forest's edge. Many live where rainfall is seasonal, so have evolved mechanisms to conserve moisture.

Exotic epiphytes fill this courtyard garden turned mini–rain forest. Jacaranda trees supply support for the plants, create a junglelike canopy, and provide the space to grow far more plants than a standard arrangement of pots on a horizontal surface.

Africa and Australia have large numbers of epiphytes, but the tropical Americas, southeastern Asia, and the islands of Indonesia have many more. In all of these regions orchids grow from sea level to the timberline, from steaming coastal forests and seasonally dry scrub woodlands to perpetually moist mist forests at the higher altitudes. Probably the highest concentrations flourish in the mountains of New Guinea and in the misty mountains of Costa Rica, Colombia, Ecuador, and Peru. Obviously, one set of growing conditions will not suit all species.

Epiphytes and lithophytes have had to adapt to receiving irregular supplies of food and drink. Many of these are orchids with pseudobulbs (see page 8). Most also have thick and fleshy leaves, whose waxy surfaces evolved to retard the transpiration of water. Some drop their leaves during rest periods and await rains to resume growth.

The roots of epiphytic orchids are also well adapted for gathering and preserving moisture, being thick, little branched, and covered by a velvety or spongy layer known as the *velamen*. This layer is made up of many cells that when dry are filled with air, but that readily take up moisture from rain or atmospheric humidity and retain it for a long time.

In addition to extracting water and nutrients, the roots of epiphytic orchids can anchor the plants on their perches. These roots have the ability to fasten onto any available support, insinuating themselves into the crevices of tree bark or clinging tightly to porous ceramic pots.

Conservatories became popular locations for orchid collections. The Como Park Conservatory in St. Paul, Minnesota, here receiving finishing touches to its restoration, was built in 1913. The worker on the dome gives an idea of its scale.

A BRIEF HISTORY

The earliest known orchids, terrestrials in the Mediterranean region, were named *Orchis*—an earthy reference to the Greek word for testicle, because of their twin oval tubers. These and other orchids from time to time have been considered useful in medicine, but the only orchid of true economic value (excepting those grown for flowers) is *Vanilla planifolia,* the source of vanilla flavoring. It was used by the Aztecs and thus became known to Europe shortly after the Spanish conquest of Mexico.

Epiphytic orchids from the West Indies and China were brought to Great Britain beginning in the 1700s; by the end of that century 15 species were growing at the Royal Botanic Gardens at Kew. Success was indifferent, however, because the plants were grown in hot, damp greenhouses with little or no air circulation.

As growing techniques improved, shortly before the middle of the 19th century, orchid growing became a craze among the wealthy and titled. Collectors canvased the tropics for new or choice orchids, sending back plants by the ton. So indefatigable were they that in many areas desirable orchids became rare or even extinct. Many plants perished in transit, still more at the unskilled hands of buyers. Prized specimens sold for enormous prices, giving rise to the perception of the orchid as a "rich man's plant." Such reckless exploitation was finally halted by a treaty known as CITES (Convention on International Trade in Endangered Species of Wild Flora and Fauna). Under its terms, international trade in endangered plants and animals has been strictly controlled.

An even greater danger, however, has been habitat destruction. The clearing of forests to harvest lumber or to create agricultural or pasture lands has seriously diminished the world's orchid population. Fires purposely set to clear land can reduce large areas to a semidesert condition; for example, they may well have obliterated many Indonesian orchid species. Fortunately, one comparatively recent development has benefited both the economies of orchid-rich but cash-poor countries and the preservation of their native species. In many countries, native orchids are now being grown in nurseries for export, for local sale, and to restock natural habitats.

Another contribution to the increased availability of orchids has been the crossing of native species. Hybridization began in the 1850s, when it became evident that orchids that rarely crossed in the wild could be induced to do so by the horticulturist. Indeed, many crosses between genera were made; the current list of hybrids far surpasses 100,000 and continues to grow with each year.

Difficulties in propagating, nonetheless, kept orchids scarce and expensive for some time. Propagation by seed was slow and chancy, so division was the only means of ensuring the increase of choice plants. Orchids remained a plaything of the wealthy until the discovery of seed germination in a sterile nutrient medium made raising seedlings practical on a mass scale. Later, tissue culture in similar media made possible the replication of selected choice specimens (see page 30).

GETTING STARTED WITH ORCHIDS

Orchid raising is a hobby that you can pursue as far as your means and time will allow. With more than 25,000 species and 100,000 hybrids, the orchid family is one of the largest in the plant kingdom, so you are not likely to run out of subjects. Still, you can be contented with a few plants on a windowsill, happy with an artificial light setup in the basement, and happier yet with a sheltered lanai, Florida room, or greenhouse to host a wider selection.

Chances are that your first orchid will be a plant you purchase at a florist's shop, an orchid show and sale, or an orchid grower's establishment. Another strong possibility is that you will be offered a plant by an orchid-loving friend who wishes to proselytize you. You may even be seduced by an orchid in a supermarket or nursery; these are increasingly important outlets.

Once you start growing orchids, your next move might be to join the American Orchid Society. This group publishes *Orchids,* a handsomely illustrated monthly magazine with a wealth of articles on orchids and their culture. Its advertisements are good sources for obtaining plants and supplies, and its bulletin boards list shows, sales, and other special events. Each year the magazine issues an almanac with the names and addresses of local affiliated groups, lists of orchid judges, meeting schedules, orchid sites on the World Wide Web, and a growers' directory of more than 300 nurseries and mail-order resources. The society's address is 6000 South Olive Avenue, West Palm Beach, FL 33405-4199.

UNDERSTANDING ORCHID NAMES

Regardless of the origin of your first orchid, be sure to discover its name and supply it with a label if it lacks one. Your supplier (if an orchid specialist) should be able to identify your plant. If you buy your first venture in a supermarket or a general nursery, it will probably be a moth orchid *(Phalaenopsis)* or a lady's-slipper orchid *(Paphiopedilum);* both are good choices, because they are tolerant of the low light found in most residential rooms. They are also the only two orchids commonly called by English names. From here on in your orchid adventures, it's all Latin!

As your collection grows you'll find that your recollection diminishes. You'll appreciate it later if you develop an early habit of marking your acquisitions. Labels should be written with waterproof, sunproof ink or a common lead pencil on white plastic, impressed on soft metal strips, or punched out on tape by an embossing labeler. (If your purchase has no name, you may be able to determine it later from an expert at an orchid show or sale.)

Continued on page 14>

This gorgeous and accommodating orchid with a striped lip is *Paphiopedilum venustum.*

A good choice for a beginner and a handsome addition to any collection, this is × *Laeliocattleya jongheana* 'Kristin' CCM/AOS.

DECIPHERING YOUR ORCHID'S HERITAGE

Orchid names can be confusing to a new convert, but a look at this chart, in conjunction with the explanations here and on page 14, will help you understand just why your orchid is called by a specific name—and will also encourage you to discover and record the heritage of other orchids you may acquire.

Keep in mind that only a small portion of the orchid family is shown in the chart on the facing page; at the genus and species levels, only a few examples are given to help you envision how the system works. Nonetheless, the levels and logic are the same for all other orchids.

Every orchid belongs, ultimately, to the immense Orchidaceae family, which is divided into subfamilies. The subfamilies in turn are divided into tribes, or alliances, which may also contain subtribes. Finally, within each tribe or subtribe, you'll discover the familiar genus, which is the "first name" of your orchid.

Each genus contains numerous naturally occurring species, but things become really interesting when orchids are crossbred between species, to produce hybrids such as *Cattleya* × Enid. And just to add to the mix, orchids can also be crossed between genera, resulting in intergeneric hybrids such as × *Laeliocattleya* Mrs. J. Leeman.

TOP LEFT: *Laelia anceps veitchiana* 'Fort Caroline' HCC/AOS
ABOVE: *Cattleya* Golden Sands 'Elizabeth Straus'
LEFT: *Laelia anceps* 'Rustic Royalty' HCC/AOS

Finally, exceptionally beautiful or unusual hybrids are given a variety or cultivar name enclosed in single quotation marks, and any awards that orchid has received are included as part of it's name.

It sounds complex, and it is—but once you've attended an orchid show or perused a mail-order catalog, you'll find that an orderly logic, agreed on and adhered to by all growers, does indeed reign in the world of orchid nomenclature.

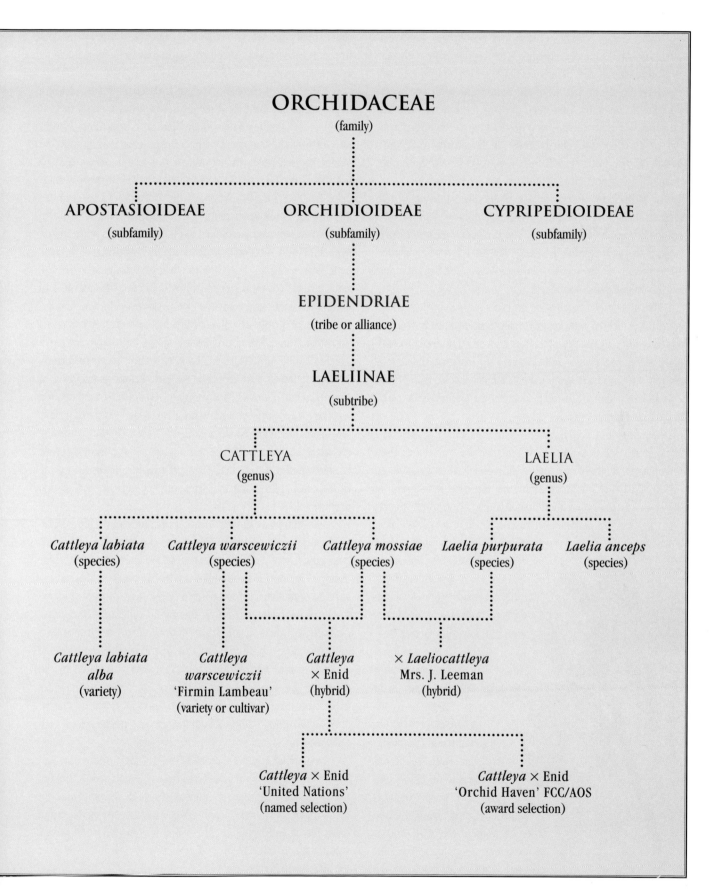

ORCHIDACEAE
(family)

APOSTASIOIDEAE
(subfamily)

ORCHIDIOIDEAE
(subfamily)

CYPRIPEDIOIDEAE
(subfamily)

EPIDENDRIAE
(tribe or alliance)

LAELIINAE
(subtribe)

CATTLEYA
(genus)

LAELIA
(genus)

Cattleya labiata
(species)

Cattleya warscewiczii
(species)

Cattleya mossiae
(species)

Laelia purpurata
(species)

Laelia anceps
(species)

Cattleya labiata alba
(variety)

Cattleya warscewiczii
'Firmin Lambeau'
(variety or cultivar)

Cattleya × Enid
(hybrid)

× *Laeliocattleya*
Mrs. J. Leeman
(hybrid)

Cattleya × Enid
'United Nations'
(named selection)

Cattleya × Enid
'Orchid Haven' FCC/AOS
(award selection)

Names are important because they are keys to plant relationships as well as to plant quality. Knowing the name is also the key to finding out your plant's needs. The chart on page 13 will help demystify the intricacies of the name game. Only one of several classifications that have been devised, the scheme on which that simplified chart is based will no doubt undergo further revision at the tribe and subtribe level. In the words of Gerard's *Herbal* (1597), "But we will leave controversies to the further consideration of such as love to dance in quagmires."

In the scheme shown in our chart, the subfamily at left, Apostasioideae, is of little importance; some botanists even exclude it from the orchid family. The Cypripedioideae subfamily contains the slipper orchids, many of which are widely grown. The subfamily at the center, Orchidioideae, contains the vast majority of cultivated orchids.

The subfamilies are divided into tribes and subtribes, which in turn are divided into genera. Each separate genus contains from one to many species that show a close relationship to each other. The genera *Laelia* and *Cattleya,* for instance, share traits that place them in the same tribe. Similarly, *Laelia anceps* and *L. purpurata,* though distinct species, are enough alike to be included in the same genus.

Stepping down to the next level on the family tree, note that although the terms *variety* and *cultivar* are sometimes used interchangeably, there is a subtle difference. When you see the word *variety* (or, more commonly, the abbreviation *var.*) in an orchid name, it means you have a naturally occurring oddball—a variation within a species. Find *Cattleya labiata alba* in the chart for a good example; this name refers to any of a number of naturally occurring white-flowering plants within the ordinarily purple-flowering species.

A cultivar, on the other hand, is in essence a single plant (or all the offspring from that plant) that has been replicated by division or tissue culture into many identical plants. (Plants grown by the latter technique are also known as mericlones; see page 30.) Cultivars are readily identifiable by the

Laelia anceps

single quotation marks around a name; any such plant that you purchase is guaranteed to be identical to its named or awarded original.

When two orchid species are crossed and the offspring made to bloom, the hybridizer gives that cross a name that all seedlings are entitled (and obliged) to bear, regardless of who else might make that cross or how many years later it might be made. For example, all hybrids of *Cattleya mossiae* and *C. warscewiczii* are called *Cattleya* × Enid. The symbol × indicates that the plant so named is a hybrid. (Don't expect to see this symbol in orchid catalogs; it is a botanist's, not a grower's, term.) You will also encounter the term *grex;* this word, taken from the Latin for flock, denotes all the offspring of a cross between two species. Keep in mind that, because plants from the same parents (or even individual plants within a species) will all differ from each other to some extent, the hybrid name is not a guarantee of quality, as with cultivars, but only of ancestry.

Really fine hybrid orchids or select individuals within a species can be further designated in two ways. The hybrid name may be followed by a selection or cultivar name enclosed in single quotation marks (for example, *Cattleya* × Enid 'United Nations' or *C. warscewiczii* 'Firmin Lambeau'). If an especially fine plant has received an award, the award initials following the name may also designate this superior plant, as in *Cattleya* × Enid 'Orchid Haven' FCC/AOS. (Awards are discussed on the facing page.) The award designation becomes a part of that orchid's name.

But wait; there's more! Members of different orchid genera, too, can be crossed freely. Plants of these intergeneric hybrids bear names that indicate their parentage: × *Laeliocattleya,* for example, denotes a cross between a laelia species and a cattleya species. Sometimes three or more genera are involved. In such instances the name may reflect the parent genera (× *Brassolaeliocattleya,* from *Brassia* × *Laelia* × *Cattleya),* or it may be a coined name established to indicate hybrid origin. These coined or code names end in *-ara* and are usually preceded by the name of the hybridizer. × *Potinara,* for instance, includes hybrids involving *Rhyncholaelia (Brassavola), Cattleya, Laelia,* and *Sophronitis.* Other examples are × *Maclellanara* and × *Bealleara.*

Notice that scientific, or Latin, names are displayed in italics; this convention is always followed in scientific works, but not necessarily in magazines or catalogs. These distinctions may not mean much to you now, when you're eager to turn the page and learn the basics of orchid care—but as your collection grows, you'll want to refer back to this section to see just how your beauties are related.

AMERICAN ORCHID SOCIETY AWARDS

While shopping in an orchid nursery or looking through a catalog, you'll often notice an abbreviation—FCC/AOS, for example—at the end of a variety's name. What does the abbreviation mean? It means the American Orchid Society (AOS) has judged that plant to be an outstanding orchid and has presented it with an award.

The AOS regularly grants these awards to exceptional plants or flowers. The society's certified judges conduct award sessions at regional conferences, regional monthly judging sessions, and annual shows. Many of the orchids pictured in this book are AOS award winners.

If you understand the criteria that AOS judges use to evaluate orchids, you'll better appreciate the orchids you see, those you want, and those you already have. This knowledge will also be useful if you decide to submit your own orchids for judging.

When considering individual flowers of new varieties, the judges evaluate form (or shape), color, size, and substance (thickness or waxiness). A round, full flower is one trait of an award winner (flatness, too, is a goal for miltonias, phalaenopsis, and vanda flowers).

Colors must be clear and definite. Multihued orchids' colors should appear in well-defined areas and patterns, and any blending of colors should be regular and harmonious, not muddy.

The new orchid's size should be an improvement over the average size of its parents. The flower's substance, too, must exceed that of the parents—a very heavy substance is the accepted ideal for some types.

An orchid deemed perfect in every respect could receive a score of 100 on the judges' point scale, though this has never occurred; for any imperfections, points are deducted. An orchid receiving 90 points or more receives a First Class Certificate (FCC), the top honor awarded by the AOS. The orchid pictured above, *Paphiopedilum* × Dollgoldii 'Oso Grande' was such a winner, as was the × *Brassolaeliocattleya* Port of Paradise 'Emerald Isle' on page 58.

A score of between 80 and 89 points earns an orchid the Award of Merit (AM). Some of the AM/AOS winners shown in this book are the *Cattleya loddigesii coerulea* 'Blue Sky' on page 57, the *Laelia tenebrosa* 'Binot' on page 62, the × *Ascocenda* 50th State Beauty 'Mayvine' on page 72, the *Phragmipedium* × Grande 'The Wizard' and the *Phragmipedium besseae* 'Laurie Susan Weltz' on page 93, the *Masdevallia* Proud Prince 'Royalty' on page 104, and the *Sobralia macrantha* 'Voodoo Priestess' on page 107.

Orchids scoring between 76 and 79 points earn a Highly Commended Certificate (HCC): this is the commendation most frequently given. Examples of recipients are the × *Laeliocattleya* 'Ontario' on page 6, the *Sophronitis coccinea* 'Vermilion Fire' on page 63, the *Odontoglossum* Castle de Ux 'Blackberry' on page 82, the *Rossioglossum grande* 'Chestnut Clown' on page 86, and the × *Burrageara* Living Fire 'Rustic Red' on page 87.

Another major award of the society is the Certificate of Cultural Merit (CCM), which is given to well-grown plants—those of good size, in prime condition, with an unusually large number of quality flowers. Because these orchids need not be outstanding new hybrids or varieties, even a beginning orchid grower can earn this award. Some examples are the × *Laeliocattleya* Canhamiana 'Mauvine Gloaming' on page 59, the *Dendrobium speciosum* 'Clay' on page 78, and the *Anguloa clowesii* 'Ruth' on page 95.

Although the immediate purpose of judging is to recognize these exceptional orchids, the American Orchid Society also grants awards to encourage worthwhile trends in hybridizing; you'll often see designations for these awards as well. The result? Better and more beautiful orchids for all of us.

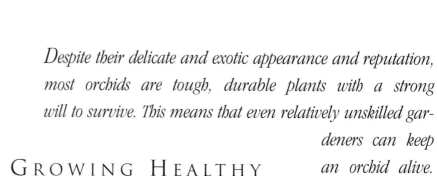

GROWING HEALTHY

ORCHIDS

Despite their delicate and exotic appearance and reputation, most orchids are tough, durable plants with a strong will to survive. This means that even relatively unskilled gardeners can keep an orchid alive. To go further— to make your orchid thrive and bloom—simply requires adherence to a few general rules and the exercise of your own common sense.

The most important factor in orchid culture is close attention to the plants; their appearance and behavior will indicate whether they are thriving. If they are not, it is up to you to recognize warning signals from your plants and remedy any deficiency. Some general rules regarding temperature, humidity, light, air circulation, and water apply to all orchids. To learn more about the needs of individual orchids, see the descriptions given in the encyclopedia listings beginning on page 53.

Advanced amateurs are likely to pursue their hobby in a greenhouse, but many orchid fanciers from every state in the Union and in every province in Canada are happily growing orchids indoors, either at a window or under artificial light.

Orchids thrive when their basic needs are met—a surprisingly easy end to achieve, if you pay attention and learn each species' likes and dislikes. These *Miltoniopsis,* for example, prefer cool temperatures.

Light through a generous window enhances a growing environment. Here, a southeastern exposure has proved just right, and leaving the windows slightly ajar allows good air circulation and prevents overheating.

TEMPERATURE AND HUMIDITY

Broadly speaking, orchids enjoy the same temperatures that we do—70° to 80°F (21° to 27°C) during the day, with a drop of 10° to 15°F (5° to 9°C) at night. As you study catalogs and talk to growers you will encounter the terms *warm-growing, cool-growing,* and *intermediate*. These all refer to a species' minimum winter nighttime temperatures—that is, the coldest conditions it will tolerate.

Cool-growing orchids, for instance, thrive in nighttime temperatures of 50° to 55°F (10° to 13°C), rising to 60° to 75°F (16° to 24°C) during the daytime. This group includes cymbidiums, odontoglossums, masdevallias, and many paphiopedilums. Some cool growers tolerate night temperatures into the low 30s (–1° to 2°C); predictably, these plants can be difficult to grow where summer temperatures are consistently high. Still, even in this group some individual species tolerate higher temperatures.

Intermediate temperatures—55° to 60°F (13° to 16°C) at night, 65° to 80°F (18° to 27°C) during the day—are satisfactory for cattleyas, dendrobiums, many oncidiums, paphiopedilums, and a large number of the so-called botanical or species orchids (see page 94). Warm growers such as vandas, phalaenopsis, and some tropical paphiopedilums appreciate nighttime temperatures of 60° to 65°F (16° to 18°C) and daytime temperatures of 70° to 85°F (21° to 27°C).

If temperatures are too high for more than a brief period, orchid plants will suffer. If bright sunlight accompanies high heat, leaves will show sunburn—bleached areas that turn brown or black. Depending on the amount of damage, the leaves may fall off or (in extreme cases) the plant may die. High heat and strong light also encourage plants to transpire, or lose moisture through their leaves, to their detriment. Even if they do not look sunburned or otherwise stressed, plants will not thrive in excessive temperatures—they will assume a yellowish tint and fail to grow or bloom.

Higher summer temperatures will not harm most orchids, however, if they are sheltered from hot sun and given increased humidity as temperatures rise. Daytime temperatures to 90°F (32°C) are actually beneficial, especially for the warm growers. Many hobbyists move their orchids outdoors for the summer, where dappled shade and moving air can reproduce the conditions they enjoy in their native forests.

Atmospheric humidity—the amount of moisture in the air—is as important as temperature to orchid health. Although most orchids grow naturally in humid environments, indoors they can make do with a humidity level of 30 to 40 percent—which fortunately is comfortable for most people as well. Lower humidity levels, like strong light and high heat, will increase their transpiration rate. To measure your atmospheric humidity, ask in hardware stores for a hygrometer.

If the humidity level is inadequate you can raise it with a portable electric humidifier, by adding a humidifier unit to your central-heating forced-air furnace, or by keeping a kettle gently steaming on the stove. As temperatures rise indoors, the humidity level should be increased in compensation. As temperatures drop in the evening so should the humidity level, in order to thwart the disease organisms that thrive in the combination of low temperatures and high humidity.

Many people maintain adequate humidity for their orchids by placing their pots on trays filled with gravel and water. Evaporation from the wet gravel keeps the air around the plants fresh and moist. Be careful not to let water in the tray rise to pot level, however; stagnant water around orchid roots will cause them to rot. Growing a number of plants close together also helps maintain humidity, because each plant's transpired moisture is shared with its neighbor.

If the indoor environment is dry, spraying your orchid plants with a fine mist of water is another way to supplement atmospheric humidity. Spray bottles of the type used for cleaning windows are easy to come by. The mist should be fine enough to leave a thin, quickly evaporating film on the leaves; a coarser spray can cause problems by drenching plant, pot, and planting mix. Spray early enough in the day so that the leaf surfaces and plant crowns can dry out before evening. This is especially important when humidifying phalaenopsis (moth orchids).

Phalaenopsis 'California Orange' HCC/AOS (TOP) is a warm grower, whereas *Anguloa clowesii* (BOTTOM) prefers cool temperatures.

LIGHT AND AIR

Light is another critical factor in growing and inducing orchid plants to bloom. In fact, lack of adequate light is the chief reason for an orchid's failure to bloom. On the other hand, too much of a good thing is a problem, as well—for instance, when it results in sunburn. And although some species require full sunlight, others need restricted light to perform well. Keep in mind that in nature, orchids seldom grow either in extremes of light or where air is stagnant. Fortunately, you can supply your indoor plants with appropriate light and ventilation, by both natural and artificial means, to keep them healthy and induce them to bloom.

NATURAL LIGHT. In your home, the amount of light a plant receives can be controlled by its placement in a window. Large east or south windows are preferred, but west-facing windows will do very well if strong afternoon light is softened with thin curtains. Bay windows can be excellent locations, and skylights and solariums greatly expand the indoor area that is well lit enough for growing orchids. Experiment: sometimes moving a plant just an inch or two—into more or less sun than it had been receiving—can mean the difference between thriving and simply existing.

HOW TO MEASURE LIGHT INTENSITY

Light intensity is measured by a unit known as the foot-candle—the amount of light cast by a candle on 1 square foot of surface. Low light is considered to be 1,000 to 1,800 foot-candles, which is equivalent to 2 hours of filtered sunlight a day. In low light conditions, a hand passed over the plant will not cast a shadow. Intermediate light, between 1,800 and 4,000 foot-candles, is equivalent to broken sunlight; your hand will cast a soft shadow on the plant. High light is considered to be 4,000 to 5,000 foot-candles, the equivalent of roughly half the strength of noonday sun; your hand will cast a sharp shadow on the plant. (Authorities disagree about exact numbers.)

When growing orchids under lights, you can duplicate natural-light conditions by adjusting the number of hours per day of light you provide and the distance you place the plants from the light source. If you are using fluorescent tubes, low light is considered equivalent to 14 hours of light daily within a distance of 8 inches from the tubes, medium light to 16 hours within 6 inches, and high light to 16 hours within 3 inches. More than 16 hours per day is actually harmful, as it can prevent flowering. If you are using other artificial light sources, you will need to adjust these times and distances somewhat; experimentation and experience will be your best guide.

If you have the equipment, there's a simple way to calculate the foot-candles of any location where you want to grow orchids. Place a sheet of plain white paper or cardboard at a 45° angle where your plant is to grow and take a reading of it with a hand-held photographic light meter.

If you don't have a light meter, a 35-mm camera with manual controls and through-the-lens metering will work. Set up the sheet of paper, then set the camera film speed at ASA 25 and the exposure at 1/60 second. Without throwing a shadow on the paper, line it up through the camera's viewfinder and take a reading by adjusting the f-stop until the needle is centered. Then convert that number to foot-candles using the following guide.

f-stop	5.6	8	11	16
foot-candles	750	1,500	2,800	5,000

On very cold winter days, move plants away from the glass somewhat. At the slightest hint of sunburn interpose a thin curtain, or move the plant back from the window or to another location where the light is not so strong. Plants that develop dark green foliage and fail to bloom may need to be moved to a brighter window.

Modern windowsills are seldom wide enough to hold any but the very smallest plants; however, wider ledges can be added to the sills or narrow tables drawn up under windows to provide "foot room" for the plants. Orchids should not be so tall as to look out of scale with the window; 30 inches is sometimes cited as the maximum height for a window plant. You will have no difficulty finding many this size or smaller. In fact, many so-called miniatures (see page 37) are less than a foot tall; two or three shelves suspended in a window may hold a dozen or more.

Greenhouse windows available as add-on structures to the house are a tempting way to gain additional space for plants, but keep in mind that the light in such windows is stronger than in conventional ones. Extra-careful attention to shading and ventilation will be needed for your orchids to prosper there.

ARTIFICIAL LIGHT. Many indoor gardeners rely on artificial lighting to replicate the conditions that their orchids need to grow and bloom. Shade-loving species, especially, often prosper under lights, and some commercial sources grow all of their plants that way.

The challenges inherent in setting up an artificial system are reproducing the full spectrum of color found in sunlight and avoiding excessive heat. Fluorescent lights were long favored for their relative coolness, which allows them to be placed quite close to plants. On the other hand, no fluorescent light supplies the entire color range necessary for both photosynthesis and bloom. A typical arrangement therefore has combined cool-white fluorescent lamps, which furnish the blue-green end and some of the orange-red end of the spectrum, with incandescents or warm-white fluorescents, which provide far-red light. (Newer, wide-spectrum fluorescent lamps can furnish 95 percent of the daylight spectrum.)

Some home growers build their own setups in a basement, attic, or other little-used space. An overhead rack might contain just fluorescent bulbs or a combination of fluorescent and incandescent bulbs. (Those less mechanically inclined can purchase racks fully equipped with shelves, fiberglass trays, lamp fixtures, lamps, and even wheels for mobility.) Orchids that like high light may be grown as close as 3 inches below the lamps. Others needing less light, such as paphiopedilums, phalaenopsis, and masdevallias, may be placed 8 to 12 inches beneath them.

MAKING YOUR OWN CORSAGES

You needn't be a florist to produce attractive professional-looking orchid corsages. With minimal supplies and as few as a dozen of your own orchid plants, selected for consecutive seasons of bloom, you can turn out corsages almost year-round.

Because of their long-lasting qualities, orchids make superior corsage flowers. The flowers are so lovely that cutting them from the plant will take courage at first, but as your collection grows the temptation to use your own flowers for special occasions and gifts will win out.

So that the flower will have developed its full color, cut it only after it has been open on the plant for a few days. Using a sterile razor, sever the flower stem from the stalk. Then, 1 to 1½ inches down from the flower base, recut the stem at an angle to enable it to take up water more readily.

Insert florists' wire (sold in most crafts shops) crosswise through the stem, close to the flower's base. Bend the wire down along each side of the stem and twist a second wire around both stem and wire, in a spiral. Using green florists' tape, securely wrap the stem and the first few inches of wire that extend beyond it; bend this extension upward. For a multiflower corsage, you can tape together several wired flowers in a pleasing arrangement. When attaching the corsage, try to pin through the tape rather than piercing the stems.

In corsages of single flowers the orchid should be worn lip side down—that is, the way it naturally grows. In multiflower corsages, at least one orchid—preferably the dominant one—should be in its natural position.

Ribbon bows can be effective complements to orchid blooms, but use them sparingly to avoid detracting from the flowers. When pinning a beribboned corsage to clothing, secure the pin through the ribbon, not through the stem.

To keep an orchid fresh for a prolonged period of wearing, the stem can be inserted in a vial of water. Tiny glass vials for this purpose (available from florist suppliers)

have a rubber cap with a hole through which you insert the unwrapped stem for its entire length. If you cannot locate the vials, you can encase the stem in moist cotton before wrapping it in plastic and disguising it with florists' tape.

Until the corsage is worn, keep it in a refrigerator where the temperature will not be lower than 45°F (7°C) — for example, in the vegetable compartment. (Stems can be left in the glass vial or moistened cotton.) Placed on a bed of shredded wax paper in a closed plastic bag, orchid flowers will remain fresh for many days.

You can easily fashion this gift to surprise and delight family and friends.

In other arrangements, the Wonderlite, an incandescent 160-watt floodlight, provides wide-spectrum light and can be positioned 3 to 6 feet above the plants. HID (high-intensity discharge) lights rated at 400 watts can be effective up to 5 feet above the plants. These are of two types: HPS (high-pressure sodium) has higher levels of the yellow, orange, and red light that boosts flowering, and is useful in the greenhouse. MH (metal halide) sheds full-spectrum, natural-looking light; it is the better choice for the home.

Most orchids thrive on 14 hours of artificial light per day throughout the year, though some need more, some less; experiment and observation are your best guides. Artificial lighting for plant growth is a complex subject; check with your local bookstores or the American Orchid Society Book Shop (see page 11) for full treatments of this topic.

VENTILATION. Free air circulation is another requirement of healthy orchids, in part because stagnant air tends to trap heat around their leaf surfaces. Home ventilation is generally satisfactory during the summer, because some windows are almost always open. In climates that require summer air-conditioning, or that prohibit keeping a window ajar in the winter, you'll need a small oscillating fan to keep air moving and help in modifying your growing conditions. Do not direct the fan at the plants, as they will not tolerate drafts; instead, position it so that the flow of air is directed above or below your orchids. If a forced-air heating or air-conditioning duct is located beneath a window where plants are growing, cover it with a deflector to direct air into the room and away from the plants.

In most climates your orchids will benefit by spending the summer out-of-doors, under light shade. The fresh, moving air and humidity are to their liking, as are the occasional cleansing rains. However, low night temperatures in the high mountains and high daytime temperatures combined with low humidity in the desert Southwest rule out summer "vacations" in locations such as these.

Paphiopedilums with all-green leaves (LEFT) tolerate cool temperatures; those with mottled leaves (RIGHT) prefer warmer conditions.

WATER

There is no single rule to tell you how often to water your orchids; most will need it once or twice a week, but that need depends on many interacting factors. A knowledge of those factors will allow you to determine the particular requirements of your plants and to make adjustments as conditions change.

Container size and type will determine the relative frequency of waterings needed, regardless of other conditions. Orchids in large pots (from 8 to 12 inches) dry out slowly; plants dry out more rapidly as the container size decreases. All potting media dry out faster in clay pots than plastic pots. Baskets and rafts or slabs require water more often than do containers with solid sides.

The type of potting medium also affects your plants' water requirements; for example, coarse fir bark dries more rapidly than does finer osmunda fiber. However, note that even when a coarse medium's surface is dry, the root area may remain moist. An easy way to determine whether a plant needs water is to poke your finger an inch into the mix; if it feels cool or moist, don't water. After you have become more familiar with your plants, you will learn to judge their moisture needs by their weight. A light plant is dry and needs water; a heavy one can wait.

The level of artificial heat indoors, too, influences your orchids' demands for water: the higher and more constant your heat, the more water they will need. Even the weather outdoors exerts an influence. On cloudy days plants cannot use up much water, because their transpiration rate is low. Conversely, on hot, sunny days they will need abundant water to replenish moisture lost through transpiration.

Here's a convenient rule of thumb: when in doubt, don't water. Remember that most orchids have their own water reservoirs in their thickened roots and leaves, so a few days without moisture will not be harmful. When watering your plants, always use tepid water—about 50° to 70°F (10° to 21°C). Cold water can actually be harmful to phalaenopsis. Other guidelines to remember are that plants in stages of active growth need more water than do resting plants, and those summering out-of-doors will need additional water to compensate for the quicker evaporation caused by breezes.

The quality of the water you give your orchids is important as well. In nature, epiphytes and lithophytes receive all their moisture in the form of rain, so most will eventually suffer or die if their irrigation water is heavily laden with mineral salts. Water passed through sodium-exchange water softeners (the kind that use salt) is especially damaging and should never be used on orchids: the process substitutes sodium for calcium, and sodium can quickly destroy orchids (and other plants, for that matter). The calcium in hard water, on the other hand, can cause lime deposits on leaves and pots, so it, too, can stunt or kill plants (except for paphiopedilums, which actually benefit from it). If your collection is small, bottled water is an option: read the label or ask your supplier for a chemical analysis.

The ideal water is rainwater, and where rain is predictable many growers go to great lengths to save it. Where public water is poor, orchid enthusiasts who don't save rainwater may remove harmful minerals from their water supply by using ion exchangers or reverse-osmosis water purifiers. (Most large water districts can furnish a chemical analysis of your water.) Where water quality is good and chlorination is the only problem, fill your watering can and let it sit overnight; the chlorine will evaporate.

HYDROPONIC ORCHID GROWING

Hydroponics is the science of growing plants in a nutrient solution. Long used for vegetable production, the technique has recently been adopted for raising orchids as well. One arrangement houses a plant in a sterile growing medium (clay aggregate) inside an ornamental double-walled pot. Water and nutrients bathe the roots in the inner pot, and an indicator shows the liquid level. The pot is relatively expensive, but the manufacturer points out that the plant needs no misting, no humidity tray, and no replacement of the growing medium. A more elaborate device is a waterproof planter containing a tank of nutrient solution. A pump automatically empties the tank into the orchid pots, and then recovers the solution for recycling. A possible drawback of this technique is that a single diseased plant can infect all others sharing the nutrient solution.

FERTILIZER

In the wild, epiphytic orchids take their nourishment from whatever comes their way in the form of falling leaves trapped around their roots, bird droppings, or nutrients dissolved in rainwater. Under these conditions their growth is slow. In cultivation they grow faster and bloom sooner if fed with fertilizers containing three basic elements—nitrogen (N), phosphorus (P), and potassium (K)—along with trace elements such as iron.

Because the coarse mixes used for most orchids drain quickly and retain little water or fertilizer, feeding must be frequent. Most orchid growers use soluble fertilizers, which are designed to be diluted with water and applied to the planting mix. Never use dry lawn or garden fertilizer; its strong concentration could destroy your plant's roots.

One common planting medium, bark, requires more nitrogen; fertilizers formulated for bark therefore follow a 3-1-1 ratio, in which the proportion of nitrogen is three times that of phosphorus and potash. Examples would be 30-10-10 or 18-6-6 formulas. The high-nitrogen formula not only furnishes enough nourishment for the plant but also satisfies the needs of the microorganisms that might otherwise consume much of the nitrogen as they slowly break down the bark.

A 1-1-1 formula contains equal parts of the basic elements and is used for orchids growing in media other than bark, or on rafts and slabs. Many orchid fanciers use a single 1-1-1 formula with success for all their orchid plants.

A third type, often referred to as a high-bloom formula, has a 1-3-2 ratio. The high phosphorus content stimulates flowering, so these fertilizers are used when growth is complete and flower bud production is anticipated.

The rule when applying liquid fertilizers to orchids is to do so lightly and frequently. (A mantra suggested by one expert is "weekly, weakly.") Follow the directions on orchid fertilizer containers to tell how much and how often. If directions are lacking or incomplete, try applying the solution in place of a watering once a week while the plant is growing and once every other week while it is resting. If the planting medium is very dry, water first; then follow up with the fertilizer solution.

If you're using a more all-purpose fertilizer, it is usually wise to dilute it to half the recommended strength but apply it twice as often as advised. Plants will, of course, need less feeding when their growth is slow, in dull winter weather, but more when they are actively growing.

Terrestrial orchids, notably cymbidiums, can be given coated slow-release fertilizer granules that will feed for many months. These come formulated to either speed growth or induce bud formation.

WHEN PLANTS NEED HELP

Any plant grown in poor conditions can fall victim to insects or disease, and orchids are no exception. However, when their basic needs are met orchids are unusually tough and trouble free.

Your greatest asset in handling plant problems will be a sharp eye for anything that seems abnormal. If you do discover a problem with an orchid, your first step should be to check the growing conditions to be sure the plant is getting what it needs to thrive. Also, ensure that the plant's leaves are kept clean and that the growing area itself is clean and free of debris.

Typical danger signs, along with their probable causes and remedies, are identified in the chart on page 27. As the same poor growing conditions are often the precursor and underlying cause of troubles involving pests and diseases, it is doubly wise to avoid them in the first place.

Proper growing conditions result in healthy plants, such as these phalaenopsis.

PEST PROBLEMS

In general, orchids are remarkably free of pests. If you do notice a problem, take care of it early to minimize its spread to other plants in your collection.

Pests that pick on orchids can be identified by the damage they do. Chewed leaves may reflect the activities of weevils, snails, or slugs. Mottled or disfigured foliage usually indicates the presence of a sucking or rasping pest: scale, aphids, mealybugs, spider mites, or thrips. Fungus gnats are primarily an annoyance, but they can also cause root rot. They thrive in overly wet and shady conditions.

Light infestations of many insects can be removed by hand with a cotton swab dipped in isopropyl (rubbing) alcohol. A solution of water and soap, water and horticultural (not dormant) oil, or insecticidal soap can be used for the same purpose. Keep in mind that insecticidal soap is most effective when applied to leaves that are already thoroughly wet; keep it away from tender buds and flowers.

If these methods prove ineffective, or if the infestation is heavy, you may need to use a pesticide. Botanical pesticides such as pyrethrin, rotenone, and neem are effective against most orchid pests. If these methods fail, you may try other, more extreme, choices, including diazinon and malathion. When using any pesticide, follow the label directions carefully and use only the amount you need.

Snails and slugs are primarily a problem in greenhouses or on plants grown out-of-doors. First try handpicking them or protecting the plant with copper strips. For severe infestations, you can use a bait containing metaldehyde, but be sure to keep it away from children and pets.

FUNGAL AND BACTERIAL DISEASES

Diseases caused by fungi or bacteria usually make the plant's tissue collapse, which frequently discolors the affected area or gives it a water-soaked appearance. Depending on the disease, the part of the plant attacked may be the leaves, stems, pseudobulbs, or roots.

Some of the more commonly encountered diseases, especially on phalaenopsis, include black rot fungus *(Phytophthora* or *Pythium)* and bacterial brown spot *(Pseudomonas)*. Both kinds will quickly kill plants, so watch for the symptoms: soft, rotted, and darkened spots on foliage.

If the plant's petals or sepals have light-colored, circular spots, it is experiencing petal blight *(Botrytis)*. This common problem can be controlled fairly easily by destroying the damaged flowers, lowering the humidity level, and avoiding splashing while watering.

Sunburn causes soft, faded spots on leaves–spots that eventually turn brown, then black. Plants taken from shaded areas and placed in sunny windows are most quickly affected.

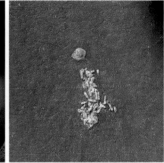

ABOVE LEFT: Mealybugs cluster on leaves and stems; try to catch an infestation when it is still light, to avoid infecting other plants.

ABOVE RIGHT: Soft scale insects create an irregular crust on the undersides of leaves and at the junction of leaf and stem.

LEFT: Aphids suck sap from stems and leaves, resulting in foliage that is mottled or discolored.

These common orchid diseases are alike in requiring high humidity to thrive. Some appear when humidity is high but temperatures low; others are not activated until temperatures are relatively high.

To discourage disease organisms, water your orchids as early in the day as possible. By the time the temperature has reached its peak the plants will be dry, remaining so as the temperature falls for the night. Keep leaf crowns and crevices free of water and try to avoid splashing the plant. Improving air circulation and avoiding plant overcrowding will also help prevent diseases.

Should any plant become diseased despite routine precautions, immediately isolate it from your other, healthy orchids. Cut out all of the diseased parts of the plant, sterilizing the tool after each cut to avoid transferring the infection to other parts or to other healthy plants. To sterilize the tool, pass the blade through a flame or dip it in rubbing alcohol or chlorine bleach. A propane torch is a readily available (and portable) sterilant. The best form of sanitation, of course, is to use a fresh blade for each cut; graphics supply stores stock various single-edged razor tools that are suitable.

Treat the cut surface with a fungicide that is formulated for use with orchids. One choice is a Bordeaux mixture (copper sulfate and lime). Other choices include topical quaternary ammonium salts, powdered sulfur, and copper preparations. Decrease both water and humidity levels while the plant is recovering.

VIRAL INFECTIONS

Viral infections in orchids take innumerable forms, but they may generally be recognized by an abnormal patterning in the leaves. This patterning—often in yellow or shades of brown, and sometimes in watery streaks—may also be expressed in the flowers. Blooms may be streaked, malformed, or exhibit colors broken into patches rather than smoothly blended; they last only a fraction of their normal life.

Viral symptoms may be obvious, or they may be subtle. Have any suspect plant analyzed by your nearest Agricultural Experiment Station or Cooperative Extension office. Check the government listings in your phone book for the office nearest you.

Unfortunately, there is no cure for viral infections; affected plants must be destroyed. Worse yet, insects and cutting tools can spread the virus to other healthy plants in a collection. Be sure to sterilize any tools that were used on the plant, as well as its container.

Suspect root rot when plants fail to grow and soft, rotted, or darkened spots appear on the foliage.

Brown rot begins as a light brown spot on the leaf and quickly spreads throughout the plant.

Bacterial leaf spot produces sunken brown spots, as on these cattleya leaves. Other kinds of leaf spot appear as yellow, brown, or reddish spots or streaks.

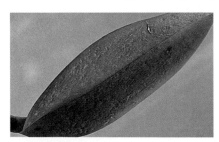

Viruses can infect many orchids, producing different symptoms in each. Here, cymbidium mosaic virus produces light pits on a cattleya leaf. The same virus causes light and dark streaks on cymbidiums.

PLANT PROBLEMS

SYMPTOM	PROBABLE CAUSE	REMEDY
Leaves turn yellow.	Too much sunlight or water. Natural if only old leaves are involved.	Give plant more shade; withhold water for a few weeks.
Leaves turn yellow and drop.	Natural with many deciduous types.	Withhold water and move plant to a cool place to encourage bud formation.
	In evergreen orchids, a sign of collapse.	See pp. 25–26 for disease control.
Leaves have black or brown areas.	Too much sun; spots that increase in size may indicate disease.	Give plant more shade; see pp. 25–26 for disease control.
Leaves are limp; growth at base of plant is soft.	Waterlogged potting mixture.	Withhold water; give plant a week with dry potting mix.
No sign of new growth.	Time is not right, in plant's growth cycle, for new growth.	Keep potting mixture evenly moist; do not force plant with extra feeding or watering.
Plant refuses to flower.	Proper growth cycle and day-length are not being observed.	Determine times of year for plant's natural growth and rest periods; keep plant in darkness at night.
	Too little light.	Gradually move plant to a brighter place.
Buds drop.	Temperatures fluctuate too greatly.	Move plant to a location with more even temperatures.
	Ethylene pollution from smog or poorly adjusted pilot light.	Check pilot lights.
Leaves have white or brown spots.	Water is too hard or high in iron content.	Leach out minerals with deionized water; use bottled water or rainwater for routine irrigation.
Leaf tips are blackened.	Too much fertilizer.	Cut back on fertilizer.
	Intense direct sun.	Move plant into area with indirect light.
	Water has high salt content.	Leach out salt with deionized water; use bottled water or rainwater for routine irrigation.
Pseudobulbs and leaves shrivel, growth slows, and roots are rotted.	Overwatering.	Reduce water.
	Poor potting mix.	Repot if potting mix has decomposed.
Pseudobulbs and leaves shrivel and growth slows, but roots are fine.	Underwatering or lack of humidity. Natural condition with many orchids.	Water thoroughly several times; increase humidity and watering frequency.

ADDING TO YOUR
COLLECTION

After you have succeeded with a few orchids, you will find that you want more; it is simply impossible to resist their beauty and variety. But before purchasing additional plants, you would be wise to plan your acquisitions. By doing so you will derive the greatest possible satisfaction for the money spent and keep disappointments to a minimum.

Of the two "rules" that you should consider when obtaining new orchids, the first is to buy only those plants that will thrive in the conditions you can offer them. If you have a warm growing area, you might concentrate on vandas and phalaenopsis. If your environment is cool, you could select miltonias, odontoglossums, and cymbidiums. Read the descriptions of these and other orchids on pages 53–108 to determine the plants' temperature tolerances.

The second rule is to buy the best plants you can possibly afford. This means avoiding unhealthy "bargain" plants as well as any that bear inferior flowers for their type. Look for plants with healthy green growth and fresh, white-tipped roots; these will be in prime shape to adjust to a new environment in your home. Healthy, mature plants will give you the most enjoyment in the least amount of time.

Cymbidiums fill a pavilion at the Santa Barbara International Orchid Show.

Hundreds of phalaenopsis fill this nursery. Commercial nurseries are a good source for quality plants and unusual specimens.

GROWING YOUR OWN

If you want to add totally different, full-grown plants to your collection, check for orchid specialists in your area or see the list of nurseries specializing in orchids on pages 40–41. Most growers are happy to offer advice in order to make you a satisfied customer. They will be able to tell you, for instance, if the orchid you want is fresh from the jungle and not yet established; in such a case they would probably suggest another, similar, purchase. If, on the other hand, you want more of what you already have, or enjoy the process of watching "babies" grow up, several methods of home propagation are available to you. They all share the advantages of costing less and teaching you more about orchid care.

Propagating plants by division, through offshoots, or by raising seedlings is easily within the realm of most home growers. The method you choose depends on the type of orchid and on how much time you want to devote to the process.

DIVIDING ORCHIDS

The easiest method of creating new orchids is by division. When you divide a plant, you'll end up with one or more new plants identical to the parent. The techniques for dividing differ, depending on the type of orchid.

SYMPODIAL DIVISION. Most orchids with a sympodial growth habit (see page 8) can be divided as you might divide an iris, to produce more plants of the same kind. Use a sharp, sterile knife to cut through the rhi-

Sympodial orchids can be separated by cutting through the rhizomes. Leave at least three pseudobulbs in each new division.

zome at a point that leaves three to five pseudobulbs or stems per division. Then carefully pull apart the mass of roots and repot each division (see page 38). Strong divisions such as these will establish themselves so rapidly that blossoms may be borne on the next year's growth.

Don't throw away orchid stems or old "back bulbs" (those pseudobulbs, taken from the rear of the plant, that no longer bear leaves); many times they can be induced to grow new shoots simply by placing them in empty pots. When growth appears, you can plant them. Plants produced in this way generally require 3 to 5 years to mature.

Clumps of paphiopedilums are easily divided into more specimens. Rather than cut the rhizome, use your fingers to break it with a twist. Leave three growths to a division. Old stems of dendrobiums can be cut into small sections and placed on moist sphagnum moss to encourage plantlets to develop. Plantlets produced naturally on the plant can be separated from the stem and potted as soon as roots form.

MONOPODIAL DIVISION. Monopodial orchids (see page 8) can also be propagated by amateurs. The side shoots that develop on many monopodial orchids can be removed and repotted once they have started their own roots. Tall-growing monopodials that make many aerial roots may be increased by decapitation: simply cut off the upper portion of the plant and plant it, with some of its trailing aerial roots, in planting mix. The lower portion will usually develop a new growing point.

Sometimes plantlets called keikis form on flower spikes, especially on phalaenopsis and the canes of epidendrums. Once their aerial roots are 1 to 2 inches long, cut or break off and pot these striplings; then enclose them, pot and all, in a plastic bag until you see evidence of vigorous growth.

MERISTEM CULTURE

Another method of division is worth mentioning, even though it is not one for the home grower. Sooner or later, you will hear or read the term *meristem culture,* which describes a specialized method of rapidly increasing the number of choice plants—especially those of a scarce new cultivar. From the plant's growing tip, the meristem (the tissues at the end of a shoot containing embryonic, or undifferentiated, cells) is removed and cultured in a nutrient solution. There it reproduces itself into masses of undifferentiated tissue. Later this material is divided into small clumps; these are set in flasks of growing media, within which they develop into seedling-size plants identical to the parent plant. Hybrids reproduced in this manner may be termed *mericlones.*

Back bulbs may produce new plants from dormant buds. Plant them when new growth appears.

Divide a tall-growing monopodial orchid by cutting off the upper portion of the plant just below the trailing aerial roots, and planting it.

Rooted keikis (Hawaiian for babies) can be cut just below the arial roots and potted.

RAISING SEEDLINGS FROM FLASKS

Growing orchids from seed is a time-consuming process best left to experienced specialists. However, you can buy flasks of small seedling plants all ready to be transferred to "community pots." This way you get the pleasure of seeing your own unique seedlings produce their first flowers, but without going through the laboratory procedures necessary for germinating the seeds.

Many orchid suppliers offer seedlings grown in flasks containing as many as 200 (but more commonly, 25 to 40) tiny plants. These plantlets are considered ready to come out of the flask when they are about ½ inch high; usually they are this size when you buy a flask. Better results can be obtained if the plantlets are bigger, however—at least 1 to 3 inches tall.

Other commercial orchid growers offer a "custom seeding service" for orchid enthusiasts who want to raise seedlings from their own parent plants but who lack the facilities to germinate the seeds. For an established fee, the grower will germinate seeds from a seed capsule that you supply; you get the seedlings back when they are large enough to be transferred from flasks to a community pot. Spring is the best time of year to do this, because it gives them the longest time to grow before any dormant period in fall or winter.

STARTING A COMMUNITY POT. A community pot is simply a more advanced "nursery" than the flask for baby seedlings; at this point they are so small—and numerous—as to make potting them individually impractical. Before removing seedlings from their flask for potting, you should assemble all of the materials you will need for the operation. A number of 3- to 5-inch pots (well scrubbed and dipped in boiling water or a 5-percent

TOP: Growing orchids from seeds begins with germination, a process usually carried out in a laboratory.

BOTTOM: This flask is filled with seedlings; a single flask may contain up to 200 tiny plants.

RIGHT: You'll have the best luck with your seedlings if you purchase a flask when the plantlets are at least 1 to 3 inches high.

bleach solution, if they have been used before) should be soaked in water for several hours so that they will not extract any water from the potting mix. When the pots are ready for use, add a potting mixture of seedling-grade fir bark combined with material you have screened out of a coarser grade. Pack the mix tightly into the pot and water it.

To remove the seedlings from the flask, pour ½ cup of room-temperature water into it. Swirl the flask; then pour out the loosened seedlings into a shallow bowl. Repeat this process until all seedlings are out.

Planting the seedlings is the easiest part of the operation. Punch holes in the potting mixture with a pencil and set several of the plants in place in their new home in the pot.

Seedlings in their first community pot require a humid location and a relatively constant temperature, in the 70° to 80°F (21° to 27°C) range. A greenhouse satisfies their needs easily. Lacking this, you can buy or easily make a small glass case to house the pots. Even a packing box with a glass pane over the top may be suitable. Whatever you use, the seedlings should be placed in a bright but not sunny spot.

Never allow the potting mixture to dry out, but remember that soggy conditions are just as unsatisfactory. You will probably have to water daily—and early enough so that the foliage will be dry by twilight, in order to thwart diseases. On sunny days the seedlings will also benefit from a fine misting during the day— again, early enough for the leaves to dry out before dusk. Open the seedlings' enclosure for an hour or two each day to allow air to circulate around the plants.

TIME TO TRANSPLANT. It will take about a year (depending on the species grown) before your seedlings are ready for transplanting (see page 38). If you started with ½-inch seedlings, put three to six plants into a clean 3-inch pot in the same type of potting mix. Give them more light and some weak fertilizer once a month.

If you began with larger seedlings, the plants are ready for individual pots whenever they start to crowd one another. Transplant them into small-grade fir bark in 2- or 3-inch containers. A final transplanting is necessary after about one more year, at which time they should go into individual 5-inch pots in medium-grade fir bark. Most plants will flower while in these pots.

If this whole procedure seems too lengthy to you, you can buy orchids in the 2- or 3-inch-pot stage. These sturdy youngsters will have passed the most vulnerable time of their lives and will be about 3 years old (that is, starting from seed); they should be about ready for their third transplanting. Depending on the vigor of the plants, a fourth potting may be needed to bring them up to blooming size.

TOP: Commercial nurseries can fill flasks with seedlings, ensuring large numbers of plants for later purchase.

BOTTOM: Freshly transplanted seedlings in a community pot (LEFT) and after 3 months' growth (RIGHT).

A PRIMER OF POTTING

Even if you eschew propagation in favor of purchasing full-size orchid plants, you'll eventually be faced with the need to repot some of your collection. Following the blooming season, and before new growth breaks, there is usually a period of 2 to 6 weeks that is optimal for repotting orchids. The plants are then in their most dormant stage, when the necessary root disturbance will be felt the least. It is also possible to transplant successfully somewhat later, when new growth is 1 to 3 inches long.

Orchids growing in 5- to 8-inch containers usually need repotting when the plants have begun to outgrow their containers and the planting medium has started to "break down" and lose its open texture. Larger plants (in larger containers) should not be disturbed for several years or until the potting material starts to lose texture. The new container you choose should be large enough to allow for 2 years' growth, but no more; this usually means a pot approximately 2 inches wider in diameter. Keep in mind that orchids do best when they are slightly crowded.

POTTING MEDIA

Most epiphytic orchids are potted in *fir bark,* which is inexpensive, comes in a variety of sizes, and breaks down slowly. The plants take nutrients from the bark as it slowly breaks down, somewhat as a time-release fertilizer capsule releases its nutrients over time. The finer the bark particles, the faster the nutrients are released. As those particles decay they also tend to pack together, reducing air spaces and thereby slowing drainage. Fine grades are used for seedlings or small plants with fine roots; they are also combined with other ingredients to make up mixes for terrestrial orchids such as cymbidiums. Larger grades are used for mature plants. The large air spaces between bark fragments ensure excellent drainage; however, bark's slow rate of decay means that the medium furnishes little nourishment, so frequent feeding is necessary.

Chunks of *coconut fiber* are somewhat similar to fir bark, but they retain water longer. This medium is far less common than fir bark, but it is plentiful in tropical areas and obtainable

Potting media, clockwise from top: tree fern fiber, rock wool, osmunda, sphagnum moss, and two types of lava rock. Fir bark, shown in the center, may be the most common potting medium.

by mail in others. (Shredded coconut fiber is being used in some areas in place of sphagnum peat moss, an increasingly scarce and ecologically threatened commodity.)

Lava rock and *gravel* do not break down at all, and they promote excellent aeration around roots—but their rapid drainage rate means you must attend faithfully to your watering. Lava rock and synthetic rock nodules retain water better than gravel does. These materials have no food value, so plants grown in them will need more frequent feeding. On the plus side, their weight makes containers more stable and less likely to fall or blow over, and these media may be sterilized and used again.

Osmunda—the tangled, matted roots of several species of ferns—was once the favored medium for epiphytic orchids, but it is now scarce and expensive. It breaks down slowly, retains some moisture while allowing free access to air, and has some food value. Although many experts still favor its use, beginners may find it harder to manage.

Perlite, or sponge rock, is seldom used alone but is a frequent element in blended mixes. It is lightweight and offers excellent retention of air as well as water. *Vermiculite* is similarly water retentive—too much so to be used alone, but useful in some mixtures for moisture-loving species. (Always use horticultural-grade vermiculite; other kinds, such as insulation grades, are too alkaline for use with plants.)

Charcoal chunks are useful for absorbing excess fertilizer or contaminants and for improving aeration, but they, too, are seldom used alone. Added to other materials in a 1-to-10 or 2-to-10 proportion, they can help maintain a healthy medium.

Sphagnum moss, live or dead, is especially useful in maintaining surface moisture for delicate roots. For that reason, it is often used to wrap the roots of orchids mounted on trees or bark slabs. Live (green) sphagnum seems to have some antibiotic and fertilizing value: New Zealand and Chilean sphagnum are the favored kinds. But beware: hard or chlorinated water will kill live sphagnum; use rainwater or deionized water with it.

Tree fern fiber—the dark, spongy, porous material used as "totem poles" to support philodendrons and similar house plants—is a well-aerated, moisture-retentive growing medium. It may be sliced into slabs for packing around roots, or plants may be attached to large pieces, which their roots will cling to or penetrate. Where tree ferns are common, whole sections of trunk are often hollowed out and used as pots.

Less common media include rock wool, styrofoam "peanuts," cork nuggets, walnut shells, and rice hulls. Rock wool is a good sterile medium, but it should be mixed with other materials to keep it from packing too tightly.

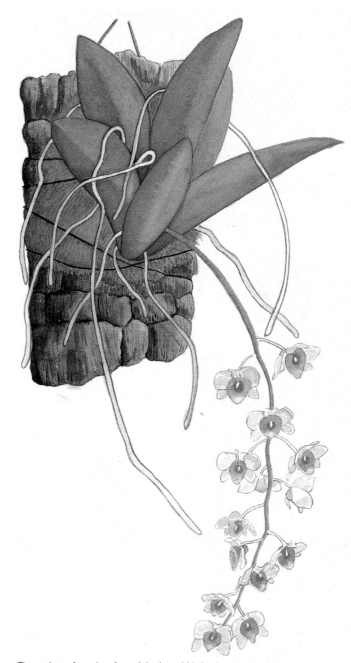

The variety of perches for epiphytic orchids is almost unlimited; tree fern fiber is one popular choice.

CONTAINERS

Most orchid enthusiasts grow their plants in pots, usually of clay or plastic: each type has its advantages. Plastic is lighter in weight and loses no moisture through its sides, thereby lengthening the period between waterings. (Glazed ceramic pots, too, restrict evaporation and require less frequent watering.) One advantage of clay pots is that their porous walls improve aeration around plant roots and—by means of evaporation from their surfaces—keep the roots cool. Their greater weight, too, helps keep top-heavy plants from falling over.

Some pots have a single hole at the bottom; others have slotted or pierced sides for faster drainage (see the examples pictured on this page). The most important criterion for any container is that it provide quick and complete drainage. Water must penetrate quickly, and air must follow the water—otherwise, the roots may deteriorate.

Those who find ordinary pots unattractive may purchase handsomely formed and glazed pots that have been designed especially for orchids. But homely pots can always be hidden inside of ornamental pots or baskets for display on the coffee table, with a thin layer of sphagnum moss on top for added disguise. Be sure, in such arrangements, not to allow the inner pots to stand in water that has drained into the decorative shell.

Wooden baskets provide extra-fast drainage for those orchids that need it; these may be suspended horizontally or—for orchids with trailing or hanging growth—vertically. Slat-bottomed baskets or rafts are essential for orchids like *Stanhopea* that send their inflorescences downward rather than upward. Orchids may also be mounted on slabs of cork bark, segments of small tree limbs, or "totem poles" of tree fern stem.

Orchid containers can be made of wood, clay, plastic, or ceramic; what they all have in common is adequate drainage.

Miniature Orchids

If you lack space in which to grow your orchids, you might investigate the miniatures. This somewhat arbitrary category includes plants like the miniature cymbidiums, which may be 2 feet tall and miniature only in comparison with their standard-size relatives, as well as others that are truly tiny—2 to 3 inches tall or even less.

Note that small size does not necessarily mean petite flowers; some miniatures have flowers startlingly large for their overall size. Some flowers are showy, in what we think of as typical orchid style, whereas others intrigue by virtue of their complexity and strangeness. Some reveal their character only when studied under a magnifying glass.

To further save space and conserve your caretaking efforts, you can plant miniature species having similar cultural needs together in one pot or on a slab of tree fern or cork bark. If shelf space is at a premium, suspend slabs in a window, taking them to the sink for watering and feeding. Or group your miniatures in trays under lights.

Here's an assortment for your consideration. For descriptions as well as the growing requirments of each one, refer to pages 53–108.

Aërangis citrata
Aërangis luteoalba rhodosticta
Angraecum distichum
Ascocentrum
Brassavola cucullata
Brassavola nodosa
Broughtonia sanguinea
Bulbophyllum barbigerum
Bulbophyllum longiflorum
Bulbophyllum medusae
Cattleya walkeriana
Cymbidium miniatures
Dendrobium bellatulum
Dendrobium canaliculatum
Dendrobium kingianum
Dendrobium trigonopus
Dendrobium unicum
Dendrochilum
Encyclia vitellina
Laelia jongheana

Laelia lucasiana fournieri
Laelia pumila
Laelia sincorana
Lemboglossum cervantesii
Ludisia discolor
Masdevallia
Maxillaria tenuifolia
Oncidium cheirophorum
Oncidium guianense
Oncidium ornithorhynchum
Paphiopedilum bellatulum
Pleione
Pleurothallis
× *Potinara*
Psygmorchis pusilla
Sarcochilus ceciliae
Sarcochilus falcatus
× *Sophrolaelia*
× *Sophrolaeliocattleya*
Sophronitis

This miniature orchid, *Laelia lucasiana fournieri,* is smaller than a pair of eyeglasses.

POTTING TECHNIQUES

Your first order of business when potting orchids is to make certain that your containers are absolutely clean. Clay pots and the broken clay shards used for drainage purposes should be scrubbed in scalding water or a 5-percent bleach solution before use. If you are planning to use osmunda, first soak the medium overnight before cutting it into 3-inch squares.

When transplanting to a larger pot, removing a plant from its old container should be done with care; live roots may be damaged if you attempt to pull out the plant by force. Soak the plant in its pot for a few minutes, and let it drain thoroughly. Then gently tap the outside of the pot with a hammer or invert the pot and strike its edge against a table top, turning it as necessary. This should free the root ball from the container. If not, you may have to break the container.

Gradually jiggle the plant out of its old potting mix; then shake off any remaining mix. The plant should be free of all old potting material. Examine the root system and trim dead roots back to living tissue. Clean out any old leaves and flower spikes and be sure the orchid is free of insect infestations. If you want to divide the plant, now is the ideal time (see pages 30–31).

POTTING IN CONTAINERS. Where you place your plant in its new pot will affect how it grows. Sympodial orchids should be placed with the oldest pseudobulbs close against the rim of the pot and with the bases of the rhizomes approximately ½ inch below the rim; the bases of the newer pseudobulbs should be parallel with the bottom of the pot, even if this means placing the whole plant at an angle. Monopodial orchids should be centered in the pot, with the bottom of the lowest leaf about ½ inch below the rim, just at the surface of the potting material.

Set the plant in place, spreading out its roots. Aerial roots that can easily be bent down into the pot should be covered by mix; others may be permitted to remain above it. Then fill in around the roots with fresh potting material, occasionally pressing it down with a blunt-edged stick. Osmunda fiber in particular should be tightly packed around the roots. Work from the sides of the pot to the center until you have filled the pot to within a half-inch of its rim. If necessary, stake the plant to hold it upright, using a soft material as a tie.

PLANTING IN BASKETS. When preparing baskets to receive orchid plants, line them with a thin layer of sphagnum and then set the plants in place as you would in an ordinary container. Ensuring adequate drainage is no problem in basket planting.

PLANTING ON SLABS. If you plan to grow your orchid on rafts or slabs of wood, bark, or tree fern, place the orchid with its roots against the slab and cover them with sphagnum moss. Tie this root ball to the slab with galvanized wire, string, monofilament fishing line, even old panty hose; or fasten it in place with electrician's staples. Keep the root ball moist; when roots appear to have securely anchored the plant to the slab, you may cut away the ties.

FOR ALL NEWLY POTTED PLANTS. After potting, set the plant in a warm location —60° to 75°F (16° to 24°C)—but out of direct sunlight. Some growers withhold water from the rooting medium, simply misting its surface and the pot's exterior. Others water freely for the first week or two to moisten the bark. Following this initial period, water sparingly. Resume normal watering only after you see that root or plant growth has started.

TOP: This rootbound cattleya has outgrown its pot.

BOTTOM: Repotting in a larger pot or even tying the cattleya to a tree will promote better growth.

POTTING ORCHIDS

1 Shake off as much of the old potting mix as possible; then cut off all dead roots, back to live tissue.

2 For a symapodial orchid, place the oldest pseudobulbs against the rim of pot and spread out the roots; divide the plant if necessary.

3 For a monopodial orchid, place the orchid in the center of the pot.

4 Add additional potting mix, tamping it in place by pressing it with your fingers or a blunt-ended stick.

5 Stake the plant to hold it upright; set it in a warm location, out of direct sunlight.

SHOPPING FOR ORCHIDS

Many general nurseries carry a few orchids for sale, but the largest and most varied selections of species and hybrids will be found at nurseries specializing in these plants. The following list includes some of the growers that publish catalogs or price lists and can ship plants to you. To obtain some catalogs there will be a small charge.

ALABAMA

GEORGE SHORTER ORCHIDS
P. O. Box 16952
Mobile, AL 36616

ARKANSAS

WHIPPOORWILL ORCHIDS
9790 Larkin Lane
Rogers, AR 72756
(501) 925-1885

CALIFORNIA

ANGRAECUM HOUSE
P. O. Box 976
Grass Valley, CA 95945
(916) 273-9426

BLOSSOMING ORCHID NURSERY
P. O. Box 96
Aromas, CA 95004
(408) 726-2429

CARSON BARNES ORCHIDS
2000 Highway 1
Pacifica, CA 94044
(650) 738-6984
fax: (650) 738-0950
e-mail: skhalsa@aol.com

CHAOTIC EXOTICS
5375 Campbell Avenue
Lompoc, CA 93436
(805) 736-0040

FORDYCE ORCHIDS
1330 Isabel Avenue
Livermore, CA 94550
(510) 447-7171
fax: (510) 828-3211

GOLD COUNTRY ORCHIDS
390 Big Ben Road
Lincoln, CA 95648
(916) 645-8600
(800) 451-8558

GUBLER ORCHIDS
P. O. Box 31200
Landers, CA 92285
(619) 364-2282

MAISIE ORCHID NURSERIES
348 North Toland Avenue
West Covina, CA 91790
(818) 237-1226
(626) 332-4599
fax: (626) 332-1168

NATURE'S TREASURES
370 Altair Way, #219
Sunnyvale, CA 94086
(408) 733-2511

ORCHIDANICA
P. O. Box 13151
Oakland, CA 94661
phone/fax: (510) 482-0408
e-mail:
orchid3@uclink4.berkeley.edu

THE ORCHID HOUSE
1699 Sage Avenue
Los Osos, CA 93402
(805) 528-1417
(800) 235-4139
fax: (805) 528-7966

ORCHIDS BY ALEXANDRA
120 Lyon Street
San Francisco, CA 94117
(415) 522-1304
fax: (415) 522-1305

ORCHIDS OF LOS OSOS
1614 Sage Avenue
Los Osos, CA 93402
(805) 528-0181

RARE ORCHIDS
P. O. Box 6332
Malibu, CA 90265
(818) 597-1389
fax: (818) 597-1380
e-mail:
orchids@ix.netcom.com

R. J. RANDS ORCHIDS
421 Westlake Boulevard
Malibu, CA 90265
(818) 707-3410

THE ROD McLELLAN CO.
914 South Claremont
San Mateo, CA 94402
(800) 467-2243

**SANTA BARBARA
ORCHID ESTATE**
1256 Orchid Drive
Santa Barbara, CA 93111
(800) 553-3387
fax: (805) 683-3405

STEWART ORCHIDS
3376 Foothill Road
Carpinteria, CA 92013
(800) 621-2450

SUNSWEPT LABORATORIES
P. O. Box 1913
Studio City, CA 91614
(818) 506-7271
fax: (818) 506-4911

ZUMA CANYON ORCHIDS
5949 Bonsall Drive
Malibu, CA 90265
(310) 457-9771

COLORADO

FANTASY ORCHIDS
830 West Cherry Street
Louisville, CO 80027
(303) 666-5432

CONNECTICUT

J & L ORCHIDS
20 Sherwood Road
Easton, CT 06612
(203) 261-3772

FLORIDA

ANN MANN'S ORCHIDS
9045 Ron-Den Lane
Windermere, FL 34786
(407) 876-2625

DABBERT ORCHIDS
1620 Melodee Lane
Englewood, FL 34224
phone/fax: (941) 475-9687

FENDER'S FLORA
4315 Plymouth Sorrento Rd.
Apopka, FL 32712
(407) 886-2464

JEM ORCHIDS
6595 Morikami Park Road
Delray Beach, FL 33446
phone/fax: (561) 498-4301
e-mail: orchids@magg.net

MIAMI ORCHIDS
22150 S.W. 147th Avenue
Miami, FL 33170
(800) 516-5348

ODOM'S ORCHIDS
1611 S. Jenkins Road
Fort Pierce, FL 34979
(561) 467-1386
fax: (561) 465-4479
e-mail:
odoms-orchids@worldnet.att.net

ORCHID ACRES
4159 120th Avenue South
Lake Worth, FL 33467
(561) 795-9190

R. F. ORCHIDS
28100 S. W. 182nd Avenue
Homestead, FL 33030
(305) 245-4570

TROPIC 1 ORCHIDS
3710 North Orchid Drive
Haines City, FL 33844
(941) 422-4750
fax: (407) 846-0281

WACAHOOTA ORCHIDS
P. O. Box 306
Keystone Heights, FL 32656
(352) 473-5504

A WORLD OF ORCHIDS
2501 Old Lake Wilson Road
Kissimmee, FL 34747
(407) 396-1887
fax: (407) 396-4177
e-mail: kricha7010@aol.com

HAWAII
BERGSTROM ORCHID NURSERY
P. O. Box 1502
Keaau, HI 96749
(808) 982-8236

CARMELA ORCHIDS
P. O. Box H
Hakalau, HI 96710
(808) 963-6184
fax: (808) 963-6125

CLOUD FOREST ORCHIDS
P. O. Box 370
Honokaa, HI 96727
(808) 987-4492

EXOTIC ORCHIDS OF MAUI
3141 Ua Noe Place
Haiku, HI 96708
(808) 575-2255

HAWAIIAN ISLAND ORCHIDS
P. O. Box 493
Waimanalo, HI 96795
(808) 259-7410

H & R NURSERIES
41-240 Hihimanu Street
Waimanalo, HI 96795
(808) 259-9626

KEN WEST ORCHIDS
P. O. Box 1332
Pahoa, HI 96778
(808) 965-9895

TROPICAL ORCHID FARM
P. O. Box 170
Haiku, HI 96708
(808) 572-8569
fax: (808) 572-8917

ILLINOIS
FOX VALLEY ORCHIDS
1980 Old Willow Road
Northbrook, IL 60062
(847) 205-9660

ORCHIDS BY HAUSERMANN
Dept. A, 2N
134 Addison Road
Villa Park, IL 60181
(630) 543-6855

INDIANA
HOOSIER ORCHID COMPANY
8440 West 82nd Street
Indianapolis, IN 46278
(317) 291-6269

MARYLAND
KENSINGTON ORCHIDS
3301 Plyers Mill Road
Kensington, MD 20895
(301) 933-0036

MASSACHUSETTS
A & P ORCHIDS
110 Peters Road
Swansea, MA 02777
(508) 675-1717

COUNTRYSIDE ORCHIDS
8 Countryside Road
Littleton, MA 01460
(978) 263-9701
fax: (978) 256-3266
e-mail: billschn@aol.com

OVID'S ORCHIDS
P. O. Box 312
Kingston, MA 02364
(508) 420-0760
e-mail: ovorc@aol.com

MINNESOTA
CASTLE ROCK ORCHIDS
P. O. Box 67
Crystal Bay, MN 55323
(612) 476-2682
fax: (612) 449-0649

GEMSTONE ORCHIDS
5750 East River Road
Minneapolis, MN 55432
(612) 571-3300

ORCHIDS LIMITED
4630 N. Fernbrook Lane
Plymouth, MN 55446
(612) 559-6425
e-mail:
orchids@orchidweb.com

MONTANA
KATZ-THOMPSON ORCHIDS
5560 Thorpe Road
Belgrade, MT 59714
(406) 388-9563

NEW YORK
BLOOMFIELD ORCHIDS
251 West Bloomfield Road
Pittsford, NY 14534
(716) 381-4206

ORCHID ART
1433 Kew Avenue
Hewlett, NY 11557
(516) 374-6426

NORTH CAROLINA
LENETTE GREENHOUSES
1440 Pom Orchid Lane
Kannapolis, NC 28081
(704) 938-2042
fax: (704) 938-7578

OWENS ORCHIDS
P. O. Box 365
Pisgah Forest, NC 28768
(704) 877-3313

SOUTH CAROLINA
CARTER AND HOLMES ORCHIDS
629 Mendenhall Road
P. O. Box 668
Newberry, SC 29108
(803) 276-0579
fax: (803) 276-0588

TENNESSEE
ELMORE ORCHIDS
324 Watt Road
Knoxville, TN 37922
(800) 553-3528

GREENHOUSE
AND
OUTDOOR
CARE

Notwithstanding the fact that orchids in bloom add great beauty to any room in your home, you may at some point decide to add a greenhouse, either to accommodate an increasingly large collection or to give your orchids the care they need while out of bloom. Your choice may be as simple as adapting a sunroom for your plants or attaching a glass lean-to against your home. It may be as elaborate as investing in a climate-controlled, multichambered structure. But whatever you choose, following the few simple rules given here for greenhouse growing will ensure success.

You may be surprised to find, too, that indulging in orchids isn't limited to growing them indoors or under glass. Many orchids can be grown successfully out-of-doors, even in cold-winter climates. Some will grow directly in the ground or attached to trees; others are better suited to containers, in which they can function as portable accent pieces. For a description of specific orchids that do well out-of-doors, see pages 48–51.

Oncidium ornithorhynchum (LEFT) and two dendrobium hybrids
flourish outdoors in this near-tropical garden patio.

ORCHIDS UNDER GLASS

Although you do not need a greenhouse to grow orchids, having a special place for them with controlled conditions is very convenient. If you begin to amass a large collection (or yearn to grow some of the larger orchids) you will certainly need one. Many plants growing together increase the humidity, and watering is easier because you needn't worry about excess water spilling over. The greenhouse may be a simple lean-to structure, a more elaborate separate building, a garden room incorporated into the house, or even a glassed-in enclosure projecting from a window. Many highly functional greenhouses have been constructed from salvaged materials. (Try checking the "boneyards" of glass and window companies for seconds or rejects of French doors and picture windows.)

If you purchase a prebuilt greenhouse, shop around before making your selection. Send for catalogs from greenhouse manufacturers to see what's available, visit any local manufacturers, and interview friends or neighbors who already own greenhouses. In cold-winter climates, greenhouses with solid walls to approximately waist height are easier to heat than all-glass houses. Partially sunken greenhouses do even more to reduce heating costs (and, for that matter, cooling costs in summer).

Five factors need to be considered when you grow orchids in a greenhouse: light, heating, humidity, cooling and ventilation, and watering. Your ability to control these interior climate factors will determine which orchids you can grow best.

LIGHT. Though plentiful light is one of the basic requirements for successful orchid culture, too much light is to be avoided. Few orchids will tolerate untempered sun year-round; leaf scorch and plant desiccation will result. Because most greenhouses are all glass, you must control the light entering by means of shades or shading compounds (such as whitewash) on the glass, especially in summer and sometimes even in winter in mild climates. One special compound provides shade in bright sunshine, becoming clear on rainy days to allow a maximum of light to enter.

Shade cloth is helpful in summer (and in winter, too, in the deep South and Southwest). Though shade cloth may be installed within the greenhouse, it is especially useful stretched on a frame above the structure. Newer greenhouse materials (corrugated fiberglass, double-walled plastics) offer adequate light with some reduction in intensity.

Orchids fill the floor and hang from the ceiling in this lovingly tended home greenhouse.

In northerly latitudes, the short wintertime day lengths may mean that additional, artificial lighting is needed, even in a greenhouse. Orchids from tropical regions are used to days and nights of equal (or nearly equal) length: balance, therefore, is as important as adequate light.

HEATING. In areas where winter temperatures regularly drop below 45°F (7°C), you'll find a heating system essential. Several heating devices are manufactured specifically for greenhouse use; the one you choose will depend on your local climate. Most greenhouse manufacturers also supply their own heating systems; study the literature

carefully to decide which unit is best for your needs. Electric heaters are useful in small greenhouses, but natural or manufactured gas is more economical in larger ones. (Gas heaters must be vented.) Thermostatic controls of varying degrees of complexity are available.

HUMIDITY. Like light, humidity is another good thing that can be overdone. Excessive humidity must be guarded against in the greenhouse: too much moisture in the air coupled with gray days is an invitation for diseases to invade. Keep humidity in the growing area between 40 and 60 percent—at

In near-tropical climates such as Florida's, orchids do well in a shade house, as shown here.

the higher end, as heat increases. Too little humidity, on the other hand, hinders plant growth and can be destructive if accompanied by high temperatures.

Several types of automatic humidifiers are available, many operating in conjunction with cooling or air circulation sys-

tems. They consist of a misting device to emit finely divided water particles, a fan to circulate moistened air, and a humidistat to measure humidity and turn both water and fan on or off. Coupled with adequate venting, these systems can also reduce the temperature inside the greenhouse.

More efficient (but much more expensive) is a fogging system, which reduces water droplets to actual fog or cloud size. Where atmospheric humidity is very low, evaporative ("swamp") coolers both cool and humidify by blowing outside air through pads of excelsior or a similar material that is kept wet by means of a circulating pump.

COOLING AND VENTILATION. Constant ventilation is essential to provide air circulation, which wafts heat away from leaf surfaces, and to avoid a stagnant atmosphere. In some instances you may need to cool the air as well as keep it moving.

Creating separate greenhouses with different climates will allow you to grow the entire gamut of orchids.

Phalaenopsis and related orchids show off well in this home greenhouse. A translucent glass roof allows just the right amount of light to reach the plants, and a heater and humidifier fit below the benches at the back.

THE WARDIAN CASE

In 1829 Dr. Samuel Ward discovered that plants could thrive in a closed box with a glazed top. Moisture, once added, transpired through the plants' foliage, condensed on the glass, and returned to the soil. The principle is the same as that of the bottle garden or terrarium. Ward's discovery was used with great success to transport plants from one part of the world to another—plants that had previously perished during long sea voyages. Victorian plant fanciers adopted ornamental versions of the Wardian case in which to grow delicate plants that required constant humidity. The original cases are rarely seen today, but a seamless acrylic tabletop version is available, and can be used indoors to reproduce greenhouse conditions on a small scale.

The simplest ventilation system is a series of vents along the roof and at the base of the greenhouse. As hot air escapes through the roof vents, cooler air will enter the lower ones. (Fans can speed up the process.) The vents can be operated manually or—if you wish to invest the time and money—automatically, by either an electric motor or a simple hydraulic cylinder device that raises the vent as the temperature increases. Bottom ventilation will also contribute greatly to the health of your orchids. Greenhouse benches, which are constructed from slats with spaces between them, will provide this important factor.

During hot summer weather, when ventilation and cooling are especially important, you may need to utilize an evaporative cooler and fan system. More elaborate systems incorporating air-conditioning are available, but are necessary only if you live in a very hot climate or plan to grow cool-temperature orchids.

WATERING. The watering frequency needs of greenhouse orchids depend on many interacting factors—not least of which is the particular orchids you grow. Basically, most orchids should be liberally watered in spring and summer but not so much during the rest of the year. Fogging or misting is always beneficial; this can be done several times a day in hot weather to keep plants cool, but is needed less during fall and winter. Never moisten plants late in the day; water standing in the leaf joints invites fungal disease.

If you water your greenhouse orchids with a garden hose, you may have to use a spray nozzle or bubbler attachment to reduce the force of the stream; a strong jet of water from the hose can wash away potting mix and expose plant roots.

ORCHID BEAUTY OUTDOORS

Gardeners in climates such as those of southern Florida and coastal California can enjoy a large number of orchids in their landscapes. Other orchids will thrive out-of-doors where winters are cold, but not so cold that the ground freezes 3 or 4 inches below the surface. Still other orchids grow naturally in some of North America's coldest climates—but these, alas, are seldom available commercially.

Orchids growing out-of-doors profit from good air circulation, natural light, and healthful dousings of rainwater. If you bring indoor orchids outside during warm weather—50°F (10°C) or above—you must accustom them to brighter light gradually, by first placing them in full shade before moving them to lighter shade for a few days. Those that can tolerate full sun (some vandas and the reed-stem epidendrums) may then be placed in the open.

ORCHIDS FOR NEAR-TROPICAL REGIONS

Southern Florida and Hawaii provide conditions favorable to the growth of many kinds of orchids. Among the favorites are cattleyas, dendrobiums, epidendrums, oncidiums, phalaenopsis, phaius, and vandas. Local growers are a good source of information about orchids adapted to such areas. Phaius, reed-stem epidendrums, and many vandas may be grown directly in the open ground, preferably in raised beds for better drainage. The soil should be amended with liberal amounts of organic material, such as sphagnum peat moss.

The other orchids mentioned above (and many more) may be grown either in containers or directly on trees. To attach them vertically, place them on a pad of sphagnum moss and tie it to the tree with copper wiring or monofilament fishing line stretched between nails driven into the tree. In time the roots will insinuate themselves into crevices in the tree bark, and the plant will support itself.

Orchids grown out-of-doors will need protection if ever frost threatens. Plants in containers can be moved into shelter; those growing on trees may be sheltered by fabric tents heated with a lightbulb.

ORCHIDS FOR TEMPERATE REGIONS

Which orchids are good risks for these gardens depends on how you define temperate. Many orchids native to high elevations in the tropics, to Japan, and to the Mediterranean regions of the world characterized by mild, wet winters and moderate, dry summers are able to withstand varying degrees of frost. Cymbidiums survive temperatures to 28°F (−2°C), but their inflorescences suffer at 32°F (0°C) and below. Tolerant of similar temperatures are Japanese calanthes; *Dendrobium kingianum, D. moniliforme,* and *D. speciosum;* reed-stem epidendrums; several laelias; *Lemboglossum cervantesii; Paphiopedilum insigne;* and some of the pleiones. These latter are even hardier: *P. formosana* can withstand brief exposure to 5°F (−15°C).

HARDY ORCHIDS

Many orchids grow wild in the cold forests and bogs of the northern United States and Canada; a few even grow beyond the Arctic Circle. Unfortunately, this does not mean that they will grow easily in all cold-winter gardens; neither does it mean that they are readily available. See the following pages for some commonly sold species that can withstand cold winters.

TOP RIGHT: *Laelia anceps* orchids provide a mass of blooms from November to March in this Southern California garden. They are also easy to care for—firmly attached to this coast live oak, they require only a spritz of water twice weekly.

BOTTOM RIGHT: A trio of miniature cymbidiums includes red Devon Lord 'Viceroy', white Showgirl 'Glamour Jane', and yellowish green Mini Mart 'Maxine'.

BLETILLA STRIATA (B. HYACINTHINA)

This native of China and Japan is the most widely available of the hardy orchids and the easiest to grow. Many bulb growers and general nursery catalogs offer it. Broadly lance-shaped, pleated leaves arise from an underground tuberous pseudobulb. Inflorescences 1 to 1½ feet tall produce up to a dozen pinkish purple flowers in late spring or early summer; a form with white flowers also exists. Flowers resemble cattleyas in shape and are 1 to 2 inches wide. The leaves remain attractive throughout summer and early fall.

Given rich, humus-filled soil in a lightly shaded or sunny place, bletillas will increase to form large colonies. Their hardiness depends on how deeply the ground freezes: Set tubers 3 to 4 inches deep in early spring. If the ground freezes to that depth or deeper in your area, dig up the tubers in fall and store them.

CYPRIPEDIUM

These native lady's slippers are related to and resemble the tropical slipper orchids (see *Paphiopedilum* on pages 89–92) but grow in colder climes. They are at once the most cherished of truly hardy orchids, the most difficult to find, and the most challenging to grow. A few diligent enthusiasts succeed with them, but many fail. These slippers resent transplanting and are fussy about both soil and exposure. Their survival may depend on their association with mycorrhizal fungi; in any case, all profit from an autumn mulch of dead leaves or garden compost.

Native plant numbers have been depleted by indiscriminate collecting, both in North America and abroad; though now protected by law, they are nowhere common. Nursery-grown plants are scarce as well. Be sure that you purchase only plants artificially propagated from seed, never wild-collected plants. In addition to the following, other species may rarely and sporadically be offered in catalogs.

Cypripedium acaule. PINK LADY'S SLIPPER, MOCCASIN FLOWER. Native from Newfoundland and Saskatchewan to Indiana, Alabama, and Georgia. Rhizomes produce a pair of leaves that rest on the ground and a 1-foot stem with a single flower. The petals are greenish or brownish, and the large inflated lip is bright pink. The plant grows in pine woods or at the edge of bogs, enjoying an acid soil. One of

TOP: *Bletilla striata*
BOTTOM: *Cypripedium acaule*

the most attractive of the native slippers, it is also the hardest to grow. Some fanciers suggest that a mulch of pine needles under the leaves will lessen the danger of soilborne fungal attack. Spring or summer bloom.

C. calceolus. YELLOW LADY'S SLIPPER. Native to much of the northern latitudes of America and Eurasia. Plants are 4 to 18 inches tall and have three to five pleated leaves clasping the stem, which bears one or two flowers with spirally twisted brownish petals and a large yellow "slipper." The tiny *C. c. parviflorum* is half the size of the species, with two to five flowers per stem. The North American form is *C. c. pubescens.* Considered to be the easiest species to grow, it thrives in light shade or (in the coolest part of its range) in full sun. Give it a fast-draining soil with plenty of organic matter. In strongly acid soils, add limestone chips. Blooms in late spring, or late summer in the coolest regions.

C. japonicum. Native to Japan and China. Each 1- to 1½-foot stem bears a pair of fan-shaped, pleated and toothed leaves up to 8 inches wide. The single flower is borne well above the leaves and can be 4 inches across. Petals are green spotted with pink, and the large lip is pink and white. Nursery-grown plants from Japan are occasionally offered in catalogs. Early summer bloom.

Cypripedium calceolus

Cypripedium reginae

C. reginae. SHOWY LADY'S SLIPPER. Native to much of the eastern and central United States and southern Canada. Where conditions are right the showy lady's slipper forms large, leafy clumps nearly a yard tall, each stem topped in spring or summer with one or two 3½-inch flowers. The sepals and petals are white, the lip pink with white markings. It requires plenty of water and a neutral or limestone soil rich in humus. It is the state flower of Minnesota.

DACTYLORRHIZA

The Mediterranean climates of Europe and the Near East offer a surprising number of terrestrial orchids, including *Orchis,* which gave its name to the family. Many of these are cultivated in Europe and Great Britain but are seldom seen in North America. Most grow from bulblike tubers, appearing in late winter and early spring and going dormant in dry summer weather. Some grow as far west as the island of Madeira and north to Great

Dactylorrhiza foliosa

Britain. One such genus is *Dactylorrhiza,* whose plants gradually expand in clumps by extending their fingerlike rhizomes. Attractive in both leaf and flower, they are offered in a number of catalogs. (Because they are handled like bulbs, they are frequently offered by bulb and hardy perennial growers.) Give them rich soil with plenty of humus and ample water throughout their growth period. They will thrive in light shade or, where summers are cool, in full sun among common garden perennials.

Dactylorrhiza foliosa. MADEIRAN ORCHID. Plants grow to 2 feet, their stems carrying four to five bright, shining green leaves. Late spring or early summer bloom consists of dense 6-inch clusters of reddish purple spidery flowers with a large lip. *Dactylorrhiza elata* and *D. praetermissa* are similar; the former can reach a yard in height, the latter 28 inches. The three species and their many hybrids are often confused in the nursery trade.

D. maculata. Resembles *D. foliosa,* but its leaves are usually spotted with blackish purple. The flowers may be white, pink, or mauve in color.

EPIPACTIS

Two species found in North America are a water-loving perennial of wide adaptability and an introduced weed, the only weedy orchid found in colder regions.

Epipactis gigantea. BROOK or STREAM ORCHID. The common name describes this plant's habitat. Whether growing in Arizona, California, South Dakota, or Texas, brook orchid always grows near water—often at the very edge of a stream. Plants form large, leafy clumps 1 to 3 feet tall, with bright green, strongly pleated, long oval leaves. Stems end in spikelike clusters of 6 to 12 flowers, each growing from a leafy bract. These flowers are not bright in color, but they are attractive when examined closely, resembling small cymbidium flowers. An inch wide, they are green and brown variously marked with pink and purple. The bloom period is spring and summer. Easy to grow if given rich soil and plenty of water, this orchid is attractive in wild or bog gardens. A selection with deep purplish red stems and leaves is called 'Serpentine Night'.

E. helleborine. Nobody plants this little orchid, but many nonetheless harbor it in their gardens. Introduced from Europe sometime in the 19th century and first noticed near Syracuse, New York, it has spread over most of the United States and southern Canada. Plants are usually single stemmed and between 8 and 36 inches in height. Their leaves resemble those of *E. gigantea,* but on a smaller scale. The inflorescence can reach 16 inches and bear as many as 24 tiny greenish and dark purple

Epipactis gigantea 'Serpentine Night'

flowers. This orchid is likely to appear in rich, leafy soil in shady gardens but can also grow in damp or dry woodland. It is not an aggressive weed and is easy to control by pulling—but the flowers merit a close look before you pull.

GOODYERA

Grown for foliage rather than flowers—and named rattlesnake plantain for their supposedly reptilian mottlings—these small orchids make ground-hugging rosettes of broadly oval, dark green leaves strongly marked in a network of white veins. The tiny white flowers come in dense spikes. These are woodland plants that like shade and a soil consisting principally of leaf mold. They occasionally grow in moss on shaded rocks. Grow them in shaded rock gardens or shaded alpine troughs. They are more readily seen if planted high on a bank or above a wall.

Goodyera oblongifolia. A native mainly of North America's western mountains, this species is also represented in the Northeast and around the Great Lakes. Its leaves are up to 4 inches long and nearly as wide; they may be plain dark green, but are usually heavily netted with silvery white. The flower spike is less than 6 inches long. Summer bloom.

G. pubescens. Native to forests in much of eastern North America, this little rattlesnake plantain is widely adaptable, asking only shade, ample humus, and moderate to heavy supplies of water to thrive. It resembles *G. oblongifolia,* but its leaves and flowers are somewhat smaller.

A NOTE ON CONSERVATION

Some orchids have become extinct in the wild; many more have become rare as their native forests are cut down for timber or for subsistence farming. The avarice of collectors has also brought some orchids to the brink of extinction. Fortunately, efforts to grow exotic orchids from seed have met with considerable success, and some formerly threatened species are now available, nursery-grown from seed or by vegetative propagation. Even some of the more difficult hardy orchids have recently been grown from seed using new laboratory techniques. It is likely that in the future artificially propagated native orchids will be sold.

This being so, there is no need to collect native orchids in the wild. Indeed, it is illegal to do so in most jurisdictions, and in any case the transplants rarely survive for more than a year. Always buy your plants from a reputable source, and inquire to ascertain that the plants offered have been propagated in the nursery and not taken from the woods.

Cypripedium calceolus parviflorum

The orchid family offers a vast range of flower and plant forms, each having specific growing needs. To start a collection, look for orchids that do well in the growing conditions you can provide.

A GALAXY OF
STAR
PERFORMERS

Even if you are just a rank beginner, you'll probably recognize the five favorites: cattleya, cymbidium, dendrobium, paphiopedilum, and phalaenopsis. Many other, less familiar orchids also make good choices at first. Experienced growers can experiment with more exotic orchids; new stars are constantly arriving on the scene.

The orchids described in this section are among the most widely grown. Many of them should be available from orchid nurseries or mail-order catalogs (see pages 40–41 for a listing); some—especially the named varieties—may require a more diligent search. Because of continuing hybridization, named orchid varieties come and go rapidly. The varieties pictured in this book are representative of the vast selection of flower colors and forms available.

A sea of orchids from many alliances floods this space with beauty.

HOW ORCHIDS ARE CLASSIFIED

Botanists divide this large family of plants into more manageable groups called alliances or tribes; orchid fanciers and growers tend to prefer the term *alliance*. An alliance consists of related genera of orchids that share some physical characteristics, often have similar growing needs, and can in many cases interbreed freely. (For more information, see "Understanding Orchid Names" on page 11.)

The orchid groups presented here are popular with beginning growers. Still, within each group you can also find more unusual orchids. It is at once the joy and the despair of orchid fanciers that newer (and often better) varieties are always appearing on growers' lists.

Orchids that belong to none of the common tribes are grouped together as "botanicals" (pages 94–108). They represent tribes that may have as few as one commonly known member.

INTERGENERIC HYBRIDS

The diversity of flower forms, colors, and sizes already present in the orchid family has not stopped growers from creating new forms, colors, and sizes to add to the collection. Hybridizers have gone beyond the comparatively subtle changes that occur when varieties and species are crossed (see page 14); they now combine desirable traits from such contrasting genera as the large, clambering *Vanda* and the compact dwarf *Ascocentrum*. The resulting intergeneric hybrid, called an × *Ascocenda*, is a small plant that yields relatively large vandalike flowers. The symbol × indicates a hybrid; it precedes the genus name in intergeneric hybrids, the species name in interspecific ones. (You will see the × consistently in botanical writings, though seldom in catalogs.)

Within the sections describing the *Cattleya* and *Oncidium* alliances, you'll find lists of some examples of intergeneric hybrids— only a small selection from the hundreds of known hybrid genera.

NEW NAMES FOR OLD ORCHIDS

You may see new, unfamiliar names for some well-known orchids in this chapter. These name changes reflect studies of contemporary taxonomists, whose task it is to clarify plant relationships. In cases in which a new name is preferable, the older, more familiar name is placed in parentheses after the new name. For example, the orchid once called *Brassavola digbyana* is now labeled *Rhyncholaelia digbyana (Brassavola digbyana)*.

Many intergeneric hybrids were originally made when the older names prevailed, however. To avoid the necessity for renaming a large number of these hybrids, taxonomists decided to let the older names stand in combinations. Thus, hybrids between *Cattleya* and *Rhyncholaelia* are still known as × *Brassocattleya* rather than *Rhynchocattleya*.

A STARTING SELECTION

Until you feel sure of yourself, it's a good idea to start with some not-so-fussy plants. Looking for the following easy-to-grow orchids will reduce your confusion when you shop for the first time. Usually, all of these are readily available and inexpensive: *Brassavola nodosa, Cattleya labiata* and its myriad of varieties and hybrids, *Cymbidium* hybrids, *Dendrobium bigibbum phalaenopsis, Encyclia cochleata, Epidendrum ibaguense, Laelia anceps, Paphiopedilum insigne, Paphiopedilum* Maudiae, and pink or white *Phalaenopsis*. Before purchasing, however, check the growing needs of these orchids to make sure you can provide the necessary conditions. Once you've gained confidence with these, you can experiment with growing some of the more demanding orchids.

Phalaenopsis 'Buena Blush' HCC/AOS

This colorful grouping of cattleya orchids shows the range of flower colors, from subtle green with a red lip to vivid purple. In front are miniature cattleyas.

THE CATTLEYA ALLIANCE

Cattleyas and their relatives are good plants for the beginning orchid hobbyist. They are showy, yet relatively easy to grow; more important to the beginner, your friends will be convinced that you really are growing orchids!

This widely available and easily grown group of orchids contains some of the showiest flowers in the family. It includes not only the familiar *Cattleya* but also the very similar *Laelia* and the highly variable *Epidendrum* and *Encyclia*. Lesser known in their own right, but valuable as parents in a complex assemblage of hybrids, are *Brassavola, Broughtonia, Caularthron (Diacrium), Rhyncholaelia,* and *Sophronitis*.

All are native to tropical America. Some grow near sea level and thrive in moist heat, but others are high-mountain plants that relish cool temperatures. All require bright light and appreciate a humid atmosphere. Most can tolerate a wide range of conditions, however, and therefore make good choices for the novice grower.

CATTLEYA

Cattleyas and their relatives are "the" orchid to the popular mind—the orchid of prom night and civic function corsages. Indeed, when we say something is orchid colored, we are thinking of the familiar pinkish purple of the old-fashioned cattleya.

Newer varieties range from white and the palest pink to yellow, orange, red, deep purple, green, and nearly blue. Flowers of some species are striped, spotted, or flushed with bronze and dark green, and many display lips of strongly contrasting colors.

× *Laeliocattleya* Alisal 'Rodeo' HCC/AOS

Although many of the 50-plus original species are available to enthusiasts willing to seek them out, most of the cattleyas on offer today are complex hybrids between several species, or even between different genera.

For cultural purposes, cattleyas can be divided into two classes. The unifoliate types have fat pseudobulbs with a single thick, leathery leaf, whereas the bifoliate types have thinner pseudobulbs topped by two or three leaves. Unifoliates have clusters of two to six large flowers with showy lips; the bifoliates have larger clusters of smaller flowers.

Cattleyas are sun lovers, and when grown indoors do best in a west or south window. They are considered intermediate in terms of their heat requirement: 55° to 60°F (13° to 16°C) night temperatures rising by 15°F (9°C) during the day. (These are winter figures; summer temperatures will be higher in warm climates.) Bifoliates do best at the higher end of that range, but all will survive at lower or higher temperatures.

At lower temperatures their growth will be slow and their flowering sparse. At consistently higher temperatures plants grow rapidly but bloom less. Occasional temperatures of 95°F (35°C) for a few hours will not harm your plants, so long as the humidity is high and air circulation good.

Pot cattleyas in bark or a bark-perlite mixture and keep containers on the small side, as the plants bloom better when their roots are confined. Overpotting—using too large a pot—is likely to result in root damage caused by an excess of damp potting mix.

Following the correct watering procedure is the key to success with cattleyas. Plants should dry out between waterings, but these need to be more frequent during warm, bright weather when plants are transpiring freely and in a state of active growth. In winter keep plants on the dry side, but not so dry that their pseudobulbs shrivel.

When watering always flood the pot until water runs from the drainage holes. To determine whether a plant needs watering, feel the planting mix; if it is cool or slightly damp, don't water. If the mix seems entirely dry an inch or so deep, water the plant; but remember that more orchids die from overwatering than underwatering. In time you will be able to judge the plant's water needs by its weight—a light pot needs water, a heavy one does not.

Feeding is best accomplished by means of a liquid plant food. Because bark contains little in the way of nutrients, feedings of plants potted in it must be frequent. Follow the directions on the fertilizer label. Generally speaking, feed twice a month in spring and summer, while growth is rapid, and cut back to once a month the rest of the year. If the planting medium is very dry, water the plants before feeding them.

Cattleya aclandiae. Bifoliate. Short pseudobulbs 3 to 8 inches tall produce two or three short (2- to 3-inch), roundish leaves. The flowers are 3 to 4 inches across, heavy in substance, and brownish green heavily spotted with dark purple. The lip is purple with dark veins and white side lobes. The highly fragrant flowers appear singly or two to a stalk and bloom in spring or early summer. This cattleya is easy to grow and a valued parent for short stature and heavy substance.

C. amethystoglossa. Bifoliate. A tall (to 40 inches) plant with clusters of six to eight (possibly many more) 4-inch, white, fragrant flowers with scattered purple spots and a purple lip. The flowers bloom in spring, sometimes again in fall.

C. aurantiaca. Bifoliate. Plants grow 10 to 24 inches with clusters of eight to twelve 1½- to 2-inch flowers. The color is bright orange, varying from yellow to nearly red. The bloom period is February to March. Easy to grow.

C. bowringiana. Bifoliate. Grows to 2 feet tall and bears five to twenty 2- to 3-inch rosy purple flowers. A blue form is a parent of *C.* Portia, a very old hybrid still used in the production of blue cattleyas. Easy to grow.

C. citrina. See ENCYCLIA CITRINA, page 61.

C. eldorado. Unifoliate. Pseudobulbs 3 to 6 inches tall are crowned by a single thick, leathery leaf to 8 inches long. The flowers are 5 to 6 inches across and white or white shaded with pale rose. The lip is rich purple, white at the base and with a yellow blotch at the throat. Some plants have pure white flowers marked only by a yellow blotch on the lip. The bloom season is summer or early fall.

C. gaskelliana. Unifoliate. Resembles *C. labiata,* with somewhat larger and paler flowers. Blooms in summer.

Cattleya aurantiaca

C. harrisoniana. Bifolate. Thin pseudobulbs 10 to 20 inches tall carry a pair of narrow 4-inch leaves. The flowers appear in late summer (and occasionally in other seasons); they are 2 to 3 inches across and purplish rose in color, with a yellow throat to the lip. Their texture is heavy. These plants are considered easy to bring into bloom.

C. intermedia. Bifoliate. Fifteen-inch plants bear two to five 4-inch flowers that are pink with whitish or purplish shading. Fragrant flowers appear in spring. Plants with strong splashings of contrasting colors at their petal tips are called *C. i.* 'Aquinii'. Many splash-petaled varieties have this plant in their ancestry.

C. labiata. Unifoliate. Experts disagree on whether this species has a number of varieties or whether those varieties should be considered species in their own right. Because of the significant differences among them, they will be treated here as separate species. *Cattleya labiata* proper has 12-inch pseudobulbs, each bearing a single 4- to 12-inch leathery leaf. Its floral clusters bear two to five 6-inch flowers of purplish pink; the deep reddish purple lip has a pale margin and a yellow throat with two white eye spots. Fall blooming.

C. leopoldii. Bifoliate. Tall, thin pseudobulbs can reach 4 feet, although they are usually shorter. The leaves, two or three to a growth, are tough, thick, and up to 5 inches long. The foot-long spike carries as many as 20 fragrant 3- to 4-inch flowers. These are greenish brown or deep brown with faint spotting and have a purple lip with a white base. The bloom season is summer.

C. loddigesii. Bifoliate. Fifteen-inch plants carry two to nine 4-inch flowers of purplish pink with a paler lip. A pure white form is *C. l. alba; C. l. coerulea* has flowers of soft lilac blue. Fall or winter bloom.

C. lueddemanniana. Unifoliate. Each 6- to 10-inch pseudobulb bears a single 5- to 8-inch leaf. Spring flowers, three to four on a spike, are strongly fragrant and up to 8 inches across. The color is pinkish purple with lighter shadings. The lip is similar, with a yellow suffusion in the throat and a pattern of deep reddish purple lines toward the tip. An especially fine white form is sometimes seen. This species likes warmer conditions than most cattleyas. The plants bloom in spring.

C. mendelii. Unifoliate. Similar to *C. labiata.* Large (7- to 8-inch) flowers are pale purplish pink, with a white lip tipped with rich reddish purple. May to July bloom.

C. mossiae. Unifoliate. Similar to *C. labiata,* with pink or purplish pink 6- to 7-inch flowers in May and June. Sometimes called Easter cattleya.

C. percivaliana. Unifoliate. Pseudobulbs to 6 inches long carry a single 4- to 10-inch leaf. Flowers 4 to 5 inches across are borne two to four per cluster. Their color is rosy lavender with a deeper-colored lip. The flowers have an odd fragrance and appear around Christmastime.

C. schilleriana. Bifoliate. Plants 4 to 10 inches tall have 6-inch leaves occasionally spotted with red. Short spikes carry one or two 3- to 4-inch fragrant flowers of a heavy, waxy texture. Colors range from olive green strongly spotted with brown to a deep purplish brown. The lip is pale yellow, heavily marked with purple. Bloom season is late spring to early summer.

TOP: *Cattleya loddigesii coerulea* 'Blue Sky' AM/AOS
BOTTOM: *Cattleya trianaei* 'Aranka Germaske' FCC/AOS

Cattleya walkeriana alba 'Diamond Bright' AM/AOS

C. schroederae. Unifoliate. Like *C. trianaei,* but with a distinctive fragrance and a more frilly lip, whose center boasts a deep orange blotch. Spring bloom.

C. skinneri. Bifoliate. Plants 12 to 24 inches high carry clusters of 5 to 19 or more 3-inch, fragrant, rose purple flowers. The variety *C. s. alba* has white flowers. One of the easier species to grow, tolerating high temperatures and dry air. Abundant in Central America, it is the national flower of Costa Rica. Blooms in spring.

C. trianaei. Unifoliate. Foot-tall pseudobulbs with 6- to 12-inch leaves carry clusters of three or four 6- to 9-inch lavender flowers, with variations from white to bluish purple. 'Aranka Germaske' is a white form. Bloom is in winter; this species is sometimes called Christmas cattleya.

C. walkeriana. Bifoliate. May bear one or two 2- to 4-inch leaves on the 6-inch pseudobulb. The one or two fragrant flowers are rosy purple and 4 inches wide. They appear on separate growths that emerge from the base of the most recently formed pseudobulb and can bloom at any time of the year. Their low stature and fragrance make them useful in the development of compact cattleyas. A popular white variety is 'Pendentive'.

C. warscewiczii. Unifoliate. Four-inch pseudobulbs carry a single 8-inch leaf. The flowers can reach 7 to 9 inches in diameter. Color is purplish pink; the deep purple lip has a bright yellow center. Bloom is in June and July.

INTERGENERIC HYBRIDS

What can be said about the thousands of named hybrids that represent over a century of selection and crossing, not only among cattleya species but between *Cattleya* and a dozen related genera? Nearly 60 of these intergeneric crosses have resulted in such popular and often-found genera as × *Epicattleya,* × *Laeliocattleya,* × *Brassolaeliocattleya,* × *Sophrolaeliocattleya,* × *Potinara,* and such oddities as × *Hasegawaara* and × *Wilburchangara.*

Only a few of these genera are widely sold, but the number of varieties and individual selections is immense. The list that follows gives the more common hybrid genera, along with the abbreviations commonly used to denote them.

× *Brassolaeliocattleya*
Port of Paradise 'Emerald Isle' FCC/AOS

Individual plants and crosses (grexes) are too many to name; a few of the more familiar crosses are mentioned. Remember that grexes are "flocks" of individuals that may vary considerably, although any member of one of these grexes is likely to be a fine plant. In addition, each grex name may be followed by a number of names set off by single quotation marks (× *Brassolaeliocattleya* Pamela Hetherington 'Coronation', for instance), which guarantees that the plant is truly superior. (See pages 11–14 for an explanation of orchid names.)

× **Brassocattleya (Bc.).** These are hybrids between a cattleya and one of several species of *Brassavola.* Those derived from *B. digbyana* (now called *Rhyncholaelia digbyana*) are distinguished by their large flowers with heavily fringed lips. A well-known grex is *Bc.* Deesse. Hybrids based on *B. nodosa* and its related species are smaller and less widely grown.

× **Brassolaeliocattleya (Blc.).** Many of the finest and most familiar cattleyas actually belong to this compound genus. Plants have been bred for full, rounded flowers with broad petals and sepals. Many have fringed lips derived from the *Brassavola* (now *Rhyncholaelia*) *digbyana* ancestor. The following are a few of the crosses whose names you are likely to encounter.

Fortune. Large, rounded, golden yellow flowers with a ruffled orange lip.

Greenwich. Chartreuse green flowers with a touch of purple in the lip.

Malworth. Large, shapely flowers of apricot yellow with pink markings on the lip.

Mem. Crispin Rosales. Large, deep lavender flowers with a deep purple lip and powerful fragrance.

Mem. Helen Brown. Pale green flowers with a purple lip; strongly fragrant.

Norman's Bay. Large, deep lavender to purple blooms with a deep purple lip.

Port of Paradise. Pale green with a ruffled lip and powerful perfume.

× ***Cattleytonia (Ctna.).*** Crosses between cattleyas (chiefly bifoliate ones) and *Broughtonia sanguinea* (see page 60) produce compact plants with long clusters of flowers in shades of pink, purple, red, or yellow.

× ***Epicattleya (Epc.).*** Flowers of moderate size are carried on tall, erect stems rising well above the foliage. Fireball has bright orange flowers on 16-inch stems. Purple Glory has deep lavender flowers on 24-inch stems.

× *Laeliocattleya* Canhamiana
'Mauvine Gloaming' CCM/AOS

× ***Laeliocattleya (Lc.).*** These resemble cattleyas in every detail. Vigorous plants have either one or two leaves per pseudo-bulb. Among the grexes that have produced show winners are Bonanza (deep lavender with two yellow eye spots), Nippon (white with a red lip), and Stephen Oliver Fouraker (white with a red lip).

× *Laeliocattleya intermedia aquinii*
'Sao Paulo'

× ***Potinara (Pot.).*** This cross of *Cattleya, Brassavola, Laelia,* and *Sophronitis* has combined the bright color and small size of *Sophronitis* with the vigor of the other three species. The resulting plants are compact and have flowers in rich shades of red, orange, or yellow. Keynote (yellow), Flameout (red), and World Venture (orange) are representative grexes.

× ***Sophrocattleya (Sc.).*** These offspring of *Sophronitis* and *Cattleya* are very small plants with bright orange, yellow, or red flowers.

× ***Sophrolaelia (Sl.).*** Crosses between *Sophronitis* and *Laelia* produce small plants with brightly colored flowers. Grexes include Gratrixiae (red), Orpetii (red or pink), and Psyche (red).

× ***Sophrolaeliocattleya (Slc.).*** Smaller growers than other cattleyas, these also appreciate cooler growing conditions. Many grexes have red flowers derived from their *Sophronitis* parentage. Widely grown grexes are Anzac, Jewel Box, Madge Fordyce, and Paprika.

BRASSAVOLA

Brassavolas are plants of generally drooping habit that are best grown attached to rafts or in baskets. Leaves, one to the pseudobulb, are narrow and roundish in cross section. Flowers are white, greenish, or ivory, and fragrant at night. Flowering occurs in summer, sometimes throughout the year. Plants like bright light and a drying-out after pseudobulbs have completed their growth. They thrive in hot climates.

Brassavola nodosa

*Broughtonia
sanguinea*

Brassavola cucullata. Each spidery 2-inch flower is carried on a drooping 6-inch stem. The lip is heart shaped and white with green tints.

B. digbyana. See RHYNCHOLAELIA DIGBYANA, page 63.

B. nodosa. LADY OF THE NIGHT. Its inflorescence rises to 6 inches above the narrow leaves. The three to five flowers are 1½ inches or more across, the petals and sepals narrow and pale green, ivory, or white. The lip is 3 inches wide, green and white spotted with maroon. It may stay in bloom throughout the year. This is a good orchid for beginners who can provide warm, sunny conditions.

BROUGHTONIA SANGUINEA

The clustered pseudobulbs are less than 2 inches tall and topped by narrow 6-inch leaves. Flower clusters to 20 inches tall are sometimes branched, bearing up to fifteen 1-inch flowers of bright red, with an ivory or yellow lip marked in bright purplish red.

CAULARTHRON BICORNUTUM (DIACRIUM BICORNUTUM)

Tall (10-inch) pseudobulbs bear strap-shaped leaves to 8 inches long. A slender erect or arching flower stalk reaches 1 foot long with ten to fifteen fragrant, 2- to 3-inch white flowers shaded in pale pink. This hybridizes with *Cattleya* to form the rarely seen × *Diacattleya*. (The hybrid uses the older plant name rather than the newer one.)

Caularthron bicornutum

Encyclia cochleata

ENCYCLIA

The large genus *Epidendrum* has been split into two genera on technical grounds, with many of the species having pseudobulbs being transferred to *Encyclia*. (Many encyclias are still familiarly known as epidendrums.) A very large genus native to Florida, Mexico, the Caribbean, and South America, its species differ widely in appearance. Most thrive in bright light and intermediate temperatures, resting after bloom and before new root and shoot formation starts.

Encyclia adenocaula (Epidendrum nemorale). The 3-inch pseudobulbs are topped by one to three leathery, foot-long leaves. Flower spikes bearing many 2- to 3-inch flowers may reach a yard in length. Their color varies from pink to deep purplish pink with dark markings; the lip is paler, with dark streaks. Blooms in spring or summer.

E. alata. One to three narrow, 20-inch leaves top the pseudobulbs. The fragrant, branching inflorescence can reach 4 feet in height, with many pale green or yellow-

Encyclia mariae

ish green flowers heavily marked with brown. The lip is white with dark red veins.

E. aromatica. Clustered pseudobulbs are topped by narrow 12-inch leaves and a branching inflorescence that can rise to 3 feet. The flowers are highly fragrant, cream or pale green with a pale lip veined in reddish brown.

Encyclia tampensis

E. citrina (Cattleya citrina). Plants grow suspended from branches in nature, and are thus best grown mounted on the underside of a branch or plaque of bark. The pseudobulbs are 2½ inches long and sheathed in grayish green, 10-inch leaves. The flowers are yellow with a deeper yellow lip, 2½ to 3 inches long, and sweetly fragrant. They do not open completely. These plants need cool, dry winters in order to bloom.

E. cochleata (Epidendrum cochleatum). COCKLESHELL ORCHID. The pseudobulbs are up to 10 inches long, topped by narrow 16-inch leaves. The flower stalk may rise 20 inches; it carries several yellow green flowers nearly 3 inches across. The inch-wide lip is at the top of the flower and is a deep blackish purple with a purple-veined white base. Flowering can be continuous over a number of months. This is a good orchid for beginners.

E. cordigera (Epidendrum atropurpureum). Short, clustered pseudobulbs 1½ inches high are surmounted by 6-inch leaves. The arching or drooping flower stalk carries several large (to 3 inches), dark purple or brown flowers with pink lips.

Encyclia radiata 'Obispo' CCM/AOS

E. mariae. Grayish green pseudobulbs are crowned by two or three grayish green to olive green 6-inch leaves. The flower spike, up to 10 inches long, is erect, arching, or pendulous, with several big (nearly 3-inch) green flowers with large white lips. This orchid likes cool, dry winters. Spring or summer bloom.

E. prismatocarpa. Pear-shaped pseudobulbs are crowned with foot-long leaves. Tall flower clusters contain many 2-inch flowers of yellowish green spotted with blackish purple. The lip is bluish purple with a white margin.

E. radiata. The fragrant, spring-to-summer flowers in 9-inch spikes are cream to greenish white, striped in purple.

E. tampensis (Epidendrum tampense). Native to Florida and the Bahamas, this plant has 2-inch pseudobulbs, narrow 16-inch leaves, and 2½-foot sprays of fragrant, tan to olive green, 1½-inch flowers with purple-veined white lips.

E. vitellina (Epidendrum vitellinum). Leaves 10 inches long at most top the 2½-inch pseudobulbs. The 16-inch rigidly erect flower stalk carries a dozen or more inch-wide orange to scarlet flowers with yellow lips. Blooms over a long period under cool conditions.

EPIDENDRUM

These plants are of two types. Those with firm pseudobulbs very much resemble *Encyclia*, which once was included in this group, and they require similar treatment. Species with tall, soft, canelike stems are terrestrial and can be planted in open-ground beds where frosts are rare and light. This second group grows freely and easily, blooming much of the year. The stems and aerial roots sometimes tangle and become untidy, but the plants put on a good show given rich, well-amended soil and ample water.

Reed-stem epidendrum

Epidendrum pseudepidendrum

Epidendrum ibaguense. Slender canes grow to 6 feet. Leaves 5 inches long form two ranks on opposite sides of the stems, which branch, root freely at the leaf joints, and even produce rooted offshoots. The leaves often turn reddish in hot sun. Large clusters of small red, orange, or pink flowers appear at the tops of the stems. Bloom can be continuous. Many color forms exist among hybrids of this species—lilac, pink, yellow, and white. Although named varieties exist, most are sold simply by color as "reed-stem epidendrums."

E. pseudepidendrum. Unbranched stems grow up to a yard in height, with two-ranked leaves in the upper half. The flower cluster at the end of the stem may be 6 inches across. Individual flowers are startlingly colored: bright green with a bright orange lip. Not as hardy as *E. ibaguense.*

E. stamfordianum. Pseudobulbs to 10 inches tall carry 10-inch elliptical leaves. The 2-foot, branching inflorescence is crowded with fragrant, 1-inch-wide yellow or green flowers spotted with reddish brown. The lip is white, sometimes flushed with pink.

LAELIA

This very large (more than 60 species and a host of varieties) genus is closely related to *Cattleya.* Flowers of the larger species greatly resemble the familiar florist's cattleyas, and some of the smaller ones display cattleya-type flowers on plants barely an inch tall. Although many are epiphytes, a number of the Brazilian species grow on rocks, taking their nourishment from mosses and their own decaying older parts.

Laelia anceps veitchiana 'Fort Caroline' HCC/AOS

These orchids are subject to intense sun and heat as well as to long periods without rain, but they do enjoy a humid atmosphere. The Mexican species *L. anceps* and *L. autumnalis* are quite hardy, growing in sheltered places outdoors along the California coast as far north as the San Francisco Bay Area. In colder climates, give them cattleya treatment.

Laelia anceps. This Mexican epiphyte has one or two 6-inch fleshy leaves on each pseudobulb. The flower spike is 20 to 26 inches long and carries three to six 4-inch fragrant flowers of pinkish lilac. Many color varieties exist, including white, deep purple, and silvery blue. *Laelia a. veitchiana* has flowers that tend toward blue. Winter bloom.

L. autumnalis. Similar to *L. anceps,* but this species blooms in autumn. The lip is pinkish white with purple and yel-

Laelia tenebrosa 'Binot' AM/AOS

low markings. The variety *L. a. alba* has white flowers with a yellow throat; 'Atrorubens' is large and very dark purple.

L. jongheana. A low grower from Brazil, with 2-inch pseudobulbs bearing a single 4- to 6-inch leaf and one or two nearly 5-inch purple flowers.

L. lucasiana fournieri (L. fournieri). A short plant (to 4 inches) bearing 1½-inch white flowers with a yellow lip.

L. pumila. A short plant (to 4 inches) with 4-inch, fragrant purple flowers.

L. purpurata. This large (to 3 feet) plant resembles a unifoliate cattleya. The inflorescence carries from three to seven or eight flowers that can reach 8 inches in width. Flowers are typically white with a purple lip, but deep purple forms are known, as well as some with a lip of rose pink (*L. p. carnea*) or blue (*L. p. werckhauseri*). The Brazilians even recognize green and yellow forms.

L. sincorana. The roundish leaves are 1½ inches long, the purple flower more than 3 inches wide. This is a good plant for beginners who can provide strong light.

L. tenebrosa. Large plants bear three or four flowers on a foot-long stem. These 6-inch flowers are bronze with a purple lip.

Laelia purpurata carnea

Rhyncholaelia digbyana

RHYNCHOLAELIA

Two orchids once included in the genus *Brassavola* comprise this genus. Plants have thick pseudobulbs and thick, gray green leaves. They grow under cattleya conditions, but like even more sunlight.

Rhyncholaelia digbyana (Brassavola digbyana). The powerfully fragrant flowers are 6 inches or more across and yellowish green in color, with a broad, white, heavily fringed lip. This lip accounts for the fringing in the hybrid genera × *Brassocattleya* and × *Brassolaeliocattleya*. (The older genus name is used to form the compounds.)

R. glauca. The fragrant flowers are 5 inches in width and white, green, or pale lavender in color, with a white lip marked in purplish red.

SOPHRONITIS

Nine species of small, cool-growing Brazilian orchids display relatively large and showy red flowers. Most bloom in autumn and winter. These are not the easiest of orchids to grow: try them in shallow, broad pots or on rafts of bark. They should never go entirely dry, but overwatering must be avoided. Reduce water in winter. They need light shade and good ventilation.

These orchids have donated their compact growth and bright color to a large group of intergeneric hybrids. *Sophronitis coccinea* is the most important species. Both the pseudobulbs and the short, fat leaves are an inch long. The inflorescence is 2 inches tall and carries one to three bright red flowers a little over an inch wide.

Sophronitis coccinea 'Vermilion Fire' HCC/AOS

Cymbidiums

If you live on the Pacific Coast, you may already know that cymbidiums are as easy to grow as camellias or roses. If you live elsewhere, choosing the right kinds and giving them some special care will ensure success.

Cymbidium Hunter's Point 'Sunset'

Easy culture and a lavish show of long-lasting flowers have made cymbidiums favorites with gardeners and commercial cut-flower growers alike. Standard cymbidium hybrids produce multiple 3- to 4-foot flower spikes from February to early May (some as early as Christmas), and each spike may contain as many as thirty 4- to 5-inch flowers. The flowers have a heavy texture and last well on the plant, for 8 weeks or perhaps more. As the cut flowers are similarly durable, cymbidiums rival cattleyas in popularity as corsages.

The plants have tightly clustered egg-shaped pseudobulbs clothed with the bases of the gracefully arching strap-shaped leaves. Unlike many orchids, cymbidiums are handsome plants even when out of bloom. All are natives of a range from Japan and India to Australia. The large-flowering kinds are native to high, cool mountains and need cool nights to produce flowers. In warm-summer, cold-winter regions, grow them outside and bring them indoors before the first frost.

Smaller Chinese and Japanese species, grown in Asia as potted plants for centuries, are gradually gaining recognition elsewhere. A few dwarf species have been instrumental in producing miniatures and hybrids with hanging flower spikes. Some of these species are warm growers that can bloom without the cool nights required by the large-flowering kinds.

The aforementioned "easy culture" does need some qualification: for one thing, the large standard cymbidiums so popular as outdoor container plants on the Pacific Coast need low night temperatures to initiate flower buds. High daytime temperatures do not disturb them so long as they are not allowed to become sunburned, but nighttime temperatures should not exceed 60°F (16°C) in the fall.

Then too, from March to October, while new growth develops and matures, these plants need frequent watering. After that their water supply may be reduced, but low night temperatures of about 45° to 55°F (7° to 13°C) remain necessary if the plants are to bloom.

The plants themselves are hardy to 28°F (−2°C), but their flower spikes are more tender and can be destroyed by frost. When low temperatures are predicted, move outdoor plants beneath a deep overhang or into a garage or shed—or else cover them with cloth or plastic, making sure that the material does not touch the plants.

Cymbidium colors have become clearer and range from reds, rusts, and yellows to pinks, greens, and white. Flower shapes also vary; orchid enthusiasts often prefer more rounded petals, like those of the green flower at top right.

Miniature cymbidium Elf's Castle

Many potting mixtures are available for these terrestrial orchids. Most are based on fine-grade fir bark blended with moisture-retaining elements such as peat moss, leaf mold, or sponge rock; some incorporate fertilizers. The most important factors in any mix, though, are fast drainage yet good water retention. Pots should, of course, drain freely. Clay pots are satisfactory, but plastic pots with drainage holes on the bottom and sides are widely used because their weight doesn't add to that of the plants, which can become very large.

Cymbidiums should have enough light during the growing season to produce yellowish green foliage. If the foliage is dark green or bluish green, your light is inadequate, and your plants may fail to bloom satisfactorily. Where plants are hardy, grow them outdoors under lath or in light afternoon shade. Many people report successfully growing plants at the edge of east-facing porches, where they get full morning sun and modified light the rest of the day.

These orchids are heavy feeders: give them a complete liquid fertilizer every 2 weeks from January through July, cutting back to once a month from August through December. Slow-release fertilizers will reduce your feeding chores; use them according to the package directions.

Because cymbidiums bloom best when their roots are crowded, transplanting is necessary only when the pseudobulbs begin to crowd the edge of the pot. The best time to transplant is just after blooming. Remove the plant from the old container; if it proves difficult to slip out, invert the container, hold it by its edges, and tap it firmly against a sturdy table, bench, or fence rail. Sift the old bark or mix out of the roots, cut off any dead roots, and trim back live roots to half their original length.

If you wish to divide plants at this time, cut through the rhizome with a stout knife or pruning shears, leaving at least three leaf-bearing pseudobulbs in each division. Do not use a pot several sizes larger when transplanting; instead, select one that will allow no more than 2 or 3 inches between the leading edge of the plant (that is, the side with the newest growth) and the side of the pot. Remember, you want to maintain those somewhat crowded conditions.

Add moistened bark or mix to the pot, tamp it down, and then hold the plant in position with one hand while dropping mix down the sides with the other. Position the plant to allow space for the leading edge, or growing point, and continue to add bark, tamping it firmly around the roots. (A blunt-ended stick is a helpful tool here.) Water lightly until new growth becomes evident; then resume watering and feeding on your regular schedule. Be sure to sterilize your tools before—and after—cutting any orchid tissue.

Leafless pseudobulbs, or back bulbs, may be used to start new plants. Each will have a small bud at its base. Stand this bulb upright when it develops visible growth. Then plant it in potting mix with the new growth at soil level. The bud will develop slowly into a foliage fan. With care, you will have another blooming plant in 2 or 3 years.

Species cymbidiums of the large-growing kind are seldom sold. The following few are sometimes available, but in general they are outshone by their brilliant hybrid progeny.

Cymbidium canaliculatum. This warm-growing Australian species has drooping clusters of 1½-inch fragrant flowers in dark reddish brown with a cream lip. These clusters can reach 16 inches in length.

C. finlaysonianum. Long (to 4 feet) sprays of tawny red flowers droop from this warm-growing native of the Philippines.

C. insigne. This native of China, Vietnam, and Thailand has yard-long leaves and flower spikes rising nearly 5 feet; its 4-inch flowers are white or pale pink, spotted with red. A cool grower, it is a parent of the large standard hybrids.

C. lowianum. Similar to *C. insigne* in size and coming from the same region, this cool grower has large, arching spikes of green flowers with red markings. It is another important parent of the modern hybrids.

C. madidum. Native to Australia, this warm grower has 2-foot clusters of brown or green, highly fragrant, inch-wide flowers. It has been used in breeding hanging-basket hybrids boasting flower clusters up to 4 feet long.

MINIATURE CYMBIDIUMS

Those who find standard cymbidiums too large and too dependent on low temperatures can enjoy the miniatures—hybrids between the big standards and several smaller species, notably *C. pumilum.* These more petite versions are easy to bring into bloom, highly floriferous, and of a reasonable size (1½ to 2 feet tall) for home decoration or the small greenhouse. The flowers are smaller than those of standards, yet profuse, and come in the same color range as that of the standards: white, pink, red, bronze, brown, yellow, and green, usually with contrasting lips. They tend to bloom earlier than the standards as well: some will bloom as early as July.

Many miniature cymbidiums were bred to tolerate warmth and will often fail to bloom when grown out-of-doors in the conditions that suit standard cymbidiums. They will thrive, however, when given the same conditions that suit cattleyas. It is always wise to check the growing requirements of a specific miniature before purchasing it.

Miniature cymbidium Golden Elf 'Sundust' is both fragrant and heat-tolerant.

TOP: *Cymbidium goeringii* 'Red Heart' CHM/AOS
BOTTOM: *Cymbidium ensifolium* 'Mitchel'

Cymbidium kanran 'Green Bean' HCC/AOS

DWARF CYMBIDIUM SPECIES

These, the orchids of classical Chinese and Japanese art, have been treasured house plants in Asia for 2,000 years. Their charm lies in their scent and form rather than size. The plants are small with very tiny, sometimes subterranean, pseudobulbs and gracefully arching, grasslike foliage. The flower spikes are erect, and the small but characteristically orchid-shaped flowers are marvellously fragrant. Their popularity is now spreading from Asia to the worldwide orchid-growing community.

Cymbidium ensifolium. The summer-blooming flower spikes, 1 to 3 feet tall, bear several 1½- to 2-inch yellow or green flowers lined in red; the lip is yellow, green, or white with red markings. These are very warmth tolerant.

C. floribundum (C. pumilum). The 16-inch flower spike is crowded with 1½-inch flowers of red or reddish brown. This spring-blooming orchid is an important parent of many miniature cymbidiums.

C. goeringii (C. virescens, C. formosanum). In Asia this is called the spring orchid, because its short stems bear a single pale green or yellowish white flower in early spring.

C. kanran. Many fragrant little flowers, which range in color from green to red, decorate this winter bloomer. Some varieties have leaves striped with white.

C. lancifolium. The leaves are relatively wide (1½ inches by 8 inches long). The foot-tall flower stalk carries up to six 2-inch flowers ranging from white to green with red veins and spots.

C. sinense (C. fragrans, C. hoosai). This, the national flower of China, has highly fragrant, deep red, 2-inch flowers on a stem 2½ feet tall. It blooms in midwinter, just in time for the Chinese New Year.

THE VANDA ALLIANCE

Phalaenopsis aphrodite
'Plantation' HCC/AOS

Members of the genus Vanda are generally lovers of heat and light, thriving best in the tropics—yet the related Phalaenopsis is not only the most popular orchid, but possibly the most popular house plant, period.

Of the many genera in the *Vanda* alliance, only a few are widely grown—but those few include some of the showiest and most attractive orchids of all.

These orchids are monopodial in growth, meaning that all growth occurs at the top of the stem, where new leaves (and often even new roots) are produced. (Branching from the base or from farther up the stem does occur in some species.) Flower stems originate between the leaves. With no pseudobulbs to store moisture, monopodials rely in nature on frequent rains and high humidity to grow and bloom—though some have thick leaves and roots that enable them to withstand some occasional drying-out.

They are found from Japan and Korea southward to India, Indonesia, and Australia, with the heaviest concentration in southeast Asia, the Philippines, and Indonesia.

PHALAENOPSIS

Probably first in importance among the alliance are the species and hybrids of *Phalaenopsis,* familiarly known as moth orchids. Their popularity springs not only from their beauty, but also from their willingness to grow and flower indoors under the same conditions that their owners like—night temperatures from 60° to 65°F (16° to 18°C), warmer days, and a modest level of sunlight.

The plants are of manageable size and are attractive even when out of flower, with broad, plump, shiny, deep green or mottled leaves. The flowers are long lasting, even as orchid flowers go, and some plants may be in bloom almost continuously. Although not large, they are among the fastest orchids to reach flowering size. They need repotting every 12 to 18 months, because the necessary frequent feeding and watering cause the potting medium to break down.

Although they adapt well to typical indoor light and temperature, phalaenopsis do need more humidity than the average home can provide. For ways to provide this humidity, see page 18. One caution bears repeating: do not spray or mist plants late in the day; water standing in the center of the plant encourages rot, especially when temperatures are low.

Moth orchid's leaves appear opposite one another and are long lived. Their thick roots grow outside of the mix as well as in it. (This is perfectly normal; mist wandering roots when you mist the foliage.) Flower stems appear from the bases of the leaves and may be erect or arching, simple or branching, with many or few flowers. On some plants the flowers all open at the same time; on others, they open slowly from base to top, with

Phalaenopsis violacea

new buds appearing as the first flowers begin to fade. When the last flower has dropped, cut the stem just below where the first flower appeared; a second spike may arise from a lower node if the plant is healthy and vigorous.

Grow plants in pots and baskets or on rafts. If you are growing the plants in a greenhouse (or outdoors in the warmest climates), the baskets may be suspended in a slanting position, or even edgewise, to ensure that moisture drains from the heart of the plant.

Plants in pots should be grown in coarse bark, to which may be added perlite and charcoal. (Young, unbloomed plants or seedlings should be grown in medium-grade bark.) They should never be permitted to go dry, but the growing medium must drain freely, and the plants must never sit in water. Plants on rafts or in baskets are often grown in sphagnum moss; these thrive in greenhouses or outdoors where temperatures are consistently warm. Phalaenopsis also do well in sphagnum moss–filled plastic or clay pots; be sure to keep the moss damp and do not allow it to go dry.

Repotting is needed when the growing medium begins to break down and lose its coarse texture, or when the plant has lost so many of its lowest leaves that a stem is visible below the leaves. The best time to repot is just after bloom.

Lift the plant and shake out the old mix. Cut out any dead roots and shorten the lower healthy ones to a length that will fit in the pot. The upper long roots should be left uncut; if not too long or brittle, they may simply be pushed into the pot. Break off any stem visible below the lowest live roots. Position the plant in the center of the pot and fill in the spaces around it with mix. The potting mixture should be firmed about the roots, but not pressed in so firmly as with cattleyas. Water sparingly until plants have resumed growth, but keep the humidity high.

Plants are propagated from seed (a task for experts) or from keikis—plantlets produced at the joints of the flower stem. Commercial growers also produce mericlones (see page 31), or stem propagations. You can recognize such plants by their three-part names—*P.* Maraldee 'Soroa Brilliance', for instance. The single quotation marks are a sign of particular merit.

The plants you buy may be seedlings; certainly they cost less at that stage. Purchasing such unbloomed plants may seem like buying pigs in a poke, but they will be attractive pigs, if not blue-ribbon material (and there is always the chance that one may be a winner). Seedling labels will show the names of the two parents, as in *P.* Baxter Carol × *P.* Carmela's Wild Thing.

Phalaenopsis schilleriana

Of the 50-odd species, only a few are regularly offered; most plants for sale are hybrids. The list that follows names species that have been of great importance in improving the race; they are available from some growers. White and shades of pink and purple are most widely seen, but yellow, red, and green are appearing in increasing numbers. Flowers are often dotted, barred, or suffused with deeper colors.

Phalaenopsis amabilis (*P. grandiflora*). An arching, yard-long flower stem produces many 3- to 5-inch white flowers whose white lips are marked with red and yellow. The leaves are dark green and glossy, up to 1 foot long. Flowering season is fall and early winter.

P. amboinensis. Flower stems 6 to 9 inches long carry one or a few 2- to 3-inch yellow flowers marked with concentric circles of reddish brown. This species blooms throughout the year.

P. aphrodite. This resembles *P. amabilis,* but has somewhat smaller flowers and blooms in spring and summer.

P. cornu-cervi. The leaves are 10 inches long and relatively narrow (1½ inches). The flower spike is unusual: branched and flattened, with opposing rows of bracts (the name means deer horned). Its flowers are small, yellow to yellow green marked with brown. The spike continues to produce flowers over a long period and should not be removed until it begins to turn brown. This species likes more light than do most phalaenopsis.

P. equestris. Several stems a year, simple or branching, carry many inch-wide, pinkish purple flowers. The blooming season is long: in favorable circumstances, lasting throughout the year.

P. gigantea. Heavy, fleshy, drooping leaves to 20 inches long by 8 inches wide give this orchid its name. Pendulous spikes to 16 inches long bear rounded yellow or creamy flowers heavily spotted with brown or maroon.

P. hieroglyphica. Several branching flower stems to 1 foot tall produce a long succession of 2-inch creamy flowers, whose pronounced brown markings resemble some form of writing. Late summer bloom.

P. lueddemanniana. Branching stems and flowers resemble those of *P. hieroglyphica,* but the flower color ranges from white strongly marked with purplish brown to a solid pinkish purple. Year-round bloom.

P. sanderiana. Simple or branching 2½-foot spikes bear flowers that are usually pink but may be white. Spring and summer bloom.

P. schilleriana. The leaves of this species are a mottled grayish green, and the branching, drooping flower stem can carry as many as a hundred 3-inch flowers of pinkish lavender. Branching flower stems and profuse bloom make it a useful parent. Flowering is in spring.

P. stuartiana. This plant resembles a smaller *P. schilleriana,* but the 2½-inch flowers are white with yellow, red-spotted centers. Winter blooming.

P. violacea. The leaves are medium to large and glossy green. The 5-inch flower stem bears a few very fragrant 2- to 3-inch flowers, which usually open one at a time. One form has purple flowers, another green or greenish white with a purple center. Summer and fall bloom.

Phalaenopsis Little Kathleen 'Susan' HCC/AOS

HYBRID PHALAENOPSIS

× *Doritaenopsis* Kelsie Takasaki 'Tiger' HCC/AOS

From the species listed above have sprung an enormous number of hybrids. At one time perfection was considered to be a plant bearing long, arching stalks with many large white flowers. Those are still popular, but newer hybrids may be smaller, with branching flower clusters in white or pale pink to deep purple. The lighter ones are sometimes spotted, stippled, or striped with contrasting colors. Yellow-flowering phalaenopsis hybrids with plain or spotted and barred flowers are currently in vogue; green and nearly red flowers are also available.

A closely related plant is *Doritis pulcherrima.* (It crosses freely with *Phalaenopsis,* the offspring being called × *Doritaenopsis.*) Its leaves are smaller and more numerous than those of *Phalaenopsis,* and the plant has a short, erect stem.

The flower stem is likewise erect, 6 inches to 2 feet tall and branching, with inch-wide flowers of deep reddish purple in the upper portion. The flowers range from white and pink to deep purple, the lighter colors often showing deeper-colored stripes. This orchid blooms in the fall. All *D. pulcherrima* hybrids greatly resemble *Phalaenopsis* and are sometimes marketed as such. They are summer and fall bloomers.

Pleasing pink blossoms of a cross between
Phalaenopsis Be Glad and *Phalaenopsis* Hilo Lip

AERIDES

These are sometimes called foxtail orchids, because their arching, drooping flower clusters closely set with flowers suggest the furry tail of a fox. The stems are erect or vinelike; they are clothed with closely set leaves in two opposite ranks and throw out many aerial roots. The flowers are individually small but impressive in the mass, and highly fragrant. You grow these orchids in baskets or pots filled with coarse bark. They thrive under the same conditions as cattleyas.

Aerides odorata. Drooping, branching plants may grow to 3 feet. Flower clusters up to 1 foot in length contain 20 or more inch-wide flowers, which range in color from white to purple; white, purple-tipped flowers are most common. *Aerides lawrenceae* is similar, and is sometimes considered a variety. Its flowers are somewhat smaller. *Aerides quinquevulnerum*—again, either a species or a variety of *A. odorata*—has white flowers tipped in bright purple. Many consider it the handsomest of the entire complex. All bloom in spring or early summer.

A. rosea (A. fieldingii). Erect stems to 10 inches produce drooping flower clusters that may reach 2 feet in length and contain as many as 100 inch-wide, fragrant, pink or white flowers spotted with purple. Bloom period is spring or summer.

Aerides odorata

×Ascocenda 50th State Beauty 'Mayvine' AM/AOS

×ASCOCENDA

These are hybrids between *Ascocentrum* and *Vanda*. Depending on the parent species used in the crosses, plants may be small or large. All are erect, with stiff spikes of flowers that range in color from yellow and green to pink, orange, and red, sometimes marked with contrasting colors. Yip Sum Wah (orange) and Meda Arnold (pink to red) are well-known grexes.

ASCOCENTRUM

These natives of India and southeast Asia resemble miniature vandas, with opposing ranks of strap-shaped leaves and dense spikes of bright flowers that stand above the foliage mass. They thrive in cattleya conditions.

Ascocentrum curvifolium. Plants to 10 inches tall produce spikes that vary in color from purple to orange and red. This species was once known as *Saccolabium curvifolium*. Spring bloom.

A. garayi. Four-inch plants produce spikes of bright orange red, inch-wide flowers at almost any time of the year. It is often sold as *A. miniatum*, a similar but rarely grown plant. Bloom may occur at any time.

EUANTHE SANDERIANA (VANDA SANDERIANA)

This *Vanda* relative (known as waling-waling in its native Philippines) is striking in its own right and valuable as a parent of many hybrids. The plants are large, with long leaves (to 16 inches) and erect spikes carrying as many as ten 4-inch flowers. These are broad and rounded; the upper part of the flower varies from white to rose and is marked by red dots; the lower portion is yellowish green heavily barred and spotted with brown. It has contributed its size, shape, and markings to a number of hybrids with *Vanda* and *Ascocentrum.* Fall blooming.

NEOFINETIA FALCATA

This tiny orchid from Japan and Korea grows 2 to 6 inches tall and branches from the base. Its leaves are ranked in opposing pairs, *Aerides*-fashion, and extend up to 4 inches. White half-inch flowers with long, thin spurs are borne as many as seven on a spike in spring and summer. They are fragrant in the afternoon and at night.

RHYNCHOSTYLIS

Like *Aerides,* these bear dense clusters of fragrant flowers and are sometimes called foxtail orchids.

Rhynchostylis coelestis. Eight-inch plants display erect clusters of white flowers tipped with blue, in summer and fall.

R. gigantea. Similar to *R. coelestis,* but with larger leaves and drooping, 15-inch clusters of white flowers tipped and spotted a deep purplish red. Blooms fall and winter.

R. retusa. Plants are up to 2 feet tall and have 2-foot drooping clusters densely packed with white, purple-spotted flowers. Spring and summer bloom.

Rhynchostylis gigantea 'Elisa' AM/AOS

SARCOCHILUS

This genus of small *Vanda* relatives is largely native to Australia, where for years its small size and attractiveness have made it a favorite with orchid hobbyists. Sarcochilus plants are becoming popular in North America, especially in climates such as that of coastal Southern California, where they can grow outdoors. Stems branch from the base, forming tufts or clumps. The flowers are small, fleshy, and have a short spur attached to the lip. All are cool growers.

Sarcochilus ceciliae. Grows to 5 inches, with six to a dozen ½-inch pink flowers on a spike just taller than the leaves. Autumn to winter bloom.

S. falcatus. Called the orange blossom orchid, this forms dense 4-inch clumps of sickle-shaped leaves with arching clusters of fifteen 1-inch-wide white, highly fragrant flowers in late spring.

S. fitzgeraldii. In Australia, this species is known as the ravine orchid. It is a relatively robust plant, growing to 2 feet. It produces multiple spikes bearing as many as fifteen 1-inch-wide white flowers with red markings at the base. Spring bloom.

S. hartmannii. This is a slightly smaller plant than *S. fitzgeraldii,* with clusters of six to twenty-five 1-inch white flowers marked with red. It is a heavy bloomer, and is one parent of the superior hybrid Fitzhart. Both are spring bloomers.

VANDA

Vandas are generally large plants with opposing ranks of flat, strap-shaped leaves and an ungainly abundance of aerial roots. Some of the species have terete (pencil-shaped) leaves; these have been assigned to the genus *Papilionanthe,* though they will be listed here under the more familiar name.

Vanda coerulea

Most of the vandas are tropical, demanding full sun, warm temperatures, and high humidity. Outside of the humid tropics they need some shade. Plan carefully if you want to add vandas to your orchid collection; most are too large to use as house plants, and some would even strain the capacity of a small greenhouse.

Vanda coerulea. This much-desired plant grows 1½ to 3 feet tall, stiffly upright on a thick stem. Closely set leathery leaves are 3 to 10 inches long. The upright or leaning inflorescence is 8 inches to 2 feet long and holds ten to twenty 4-inch flat, round flowers that range from pale to deep blue. Long-lasting flowers come at any time from fall to spring. Grow this vanda with cool-growing orchids or in a cool corner of the cattleya greenhouse. This plant crossed with *Euanthe sanderiana* produced one of the more famous hybrids in orchid history, *Vanda* (properly *Vandanthe*) Rothschildiana, whose large blue flowers are checkered in a deeper blue.

V. (Papilionanthe) hookeriana. A vigorous, sprawling plant over 6 feet tall, it has terete leaves and flower clusters up to 1 foot long. These bear up to two dozen 2½-inch white and purple flowers with a large lip. Fall blooming. Both this and *V. teres* are tough, hardy outdoor plants, but not beyond the tropics.

V. (Papilionanthe) teres. This sprawling terete-leafed plant is a constant producer of 2- to 4-inch white or cream-colored flowers blending to rose or red, with a red-spotted yellow lip. A hybrid between this vanda and *V. hookeriana* is *V.* Miss Joaquim, widely grown in Hawaii as a cut flower and for leis.

Vanda tricolor

V. tricolor. Three-foot plants display clusters of fragrant, 3-inch white or pale yellow flowers spotted with reddish brown. The lip is purple and white with reddish brown streaks. *Vanda t. suavis (V. suavis)* is similar, but its spots are fewer and are reddish purple in color.

THE DENDROBIUM ALLIANCE

The dendrobiums vary widely in appearance and cultural needs, but when well grown they are among the showiest of orchids. To succeed with them, try to learn about their requirements before you buy them. If you do not, you may wait a long time for yours to bloom.

The dendrobium tribe includes only four genera, three of which are not widely grown. The fourth, *Dendrobium,* more than compensates with its enormous number of species; estimates range from 900 to 1,400 or even more. Natives grow from India, China, and Japan through Indonesia to Australia, New Zealand, and the islands of the Pacific.

These orchids are highly variable in size and appearance; the largest are 10 feet or more in height, whereas the smallest require a magnifying glass to detect the flowers. The flower colors include white, cream, yellow, orange, pink, red, lavender, purple, and blue—plus almost any conceivable combination of these. Dendrobium habitats include mountainous monsoon-region forests, tropical highlands, steaming jungles, and pine forests. Practically all dendrobiums are epiphytes, though a few are lithophytic, living in pockets of moss and leaf mold on rocks and cliffs.

Although some species possess fat pseudobulbs, most have thin, erect or pendent stems called canes. These emerge from a rhizome, but are usually tightly clumped together. Inflorescences bearing from 1 to 100 or more flowers arise from the upper portions of the cane. Plants thrive in small pots, so need infrequent repotting.

Their basic requirements are plenty of light and free air circulation. If you grow them in the house, give them an east window or a west or south window covered with thin curtains. Keep the humidity up with misting or by positioning plants above trays of wet gravel.

Given their wide natural range and highly varied structure, it follows that not all dendrobiums will thrive under the same conditions. The species mentioned here fall into one of two classes. The first, the cool-growing species, are generally deciduous. Water and feed these during growth; then allow plants a decided winter rest, with either no water or just enough to keep the canes from shriveling. During their rest, they appreciate cool nights of about 40° to 50°F (4° to 10°C). The warm-growing species are generally evergreen and require water throughout the year, though they will need somewhat less in winter.

The following species are merely a selection of the 100 or more dendrobiums currently offered by growers. Many schemes exist for classifying the dendrobiums and establishing cultural requirements for the classes; our division into warm and cool growers has the advantage of simplicity.

Dendrobium chrysotoxum

Dendrobium amethystoglossum. Cool-growing. Yard-tall canes produce drooping, dense clusters of white flowers with purple lips.

D. anosmum. Cool-growing. Arching or drooping 2- to 4-foot canes produce pairs of 3- to 4-inch rich purple, fragrant flowers in spring along the leafless canes.

D. antennatum. Warm-growing. This is one of the so-called antelope horn orchids, characterized by narrow, upstanding, often twisted sepals that resemble horns. Canes reach 4 feet and bear clusters of up to 15 fragrant white and green flowers with purple lips. Bloom is usually in winter or spring, but may come at any time.

D. aphyllum (D. pierardii). Cool-growing. Drooping, leafy stems are 3 to 5 feet long. When leaves drop, short clusters of white or purplish pink 2-inch flowers with yellow, purple-lined lips appear. Spring or early summer bloom.

D. atroviolaceum. Warm-growing. Foot-tall slender pseudobulbs bear a few leathery evergreen leaves at the top. Flower clusters bear 8 to 12 or more very long-lasting, fragrant, 3-inch, cream-colored flowers spotted with purple, with a lip heavily veined in purple.

D. bellatulum. Warm-growing. The 4-inch pseudobulbs bear two to four leathery, gray green leaves. Creamy white 2-inch flowers with yellow and scarlet lips are fragrant and long lasting. Late winter or early spring bloom.

D. bigibbum. Warm-growing. This species from Australia and New Guinea is quite variable. *Dendrobium b. bigibbum* has small (2 inches wide), light purple flowers, often with a white patch on the lip. *Dendrobium b. compactum* bears canes that reach only 10 inches, whereas *D. b. phalaenopsis* (*D. phalaenopsis*) has 3-inch deep purple flowers on canes that can be a yard tall. The latter is the most widely grown of the three. Its arching spikes grow to 10 inches or more in length and can carry as many as 20 flowers. With

Dendrobium cuthbertsonii 'Pumpkin Pie' CCM/AOS

their broad, rounded form, these look like the flowers of *Phalaenopsis,* the moth orchid. This plant, its white and bicolored variants, and a host of hybrids are among the most commonly grown orchids. Sprays of flowers ranging from white through pink and lavender to the deepest reddish purple are staples of the florist's trade. The species blooms in fall; the hybrids can bloom nearly any time.

D. canaliculatum. Warm-growing. Pseudobulbs to 6 inches tall are tapered at each end and carry several leaves toward the tip. The 4- to 16-inch-tall flower clusters bear 2-inch "antelope horn" flowers with greenish white, somewhat twisted segments and a lip marked with purple. Spring bloom.

D. chrysanthum. Cool-growing. Trailing canes can be an astonishing 6 to 8 feet long; they may be supported beneath the greenhouse roof with ties every 2 feet. Leaves drop gradually from base to tip. Clusters of one to three fragrant, golden yellow flowers 1½ inches wide arise toward the cane tips. The flowers' lips have two large, chestnut brown eye spots.

D. chrysotoxum. Cool-growing. Canes reach 20 inches and produce drooping spikes of fragrant, 2-inch golden yellow flowers in spring. The lip is fringed and has a deep orange center. Both old and new pseudobulbs bloom.

D. cuthbertsonii (D. sophronites). Cool-growing. Native to the high mountains of New Guinea, this species is a challenge even for the expert to grow. The 2-inch-tall plants have thick, dark green, inch-long leaves covered with tiny, wartlike projections. The long-lasting (to 6 months) flowers are 1 to 1½ inches wide and bright red, orange, or yellow. This plant is unusual in needing constantly cool, moist, moving air year-round to succeed. Some experts have nonetheless grown it successfully along with cattleyas.

D. dearei. Warm-growing. Erect, leafy canes 1 to 3 feet tall bear clusters

Dendrobium densiflorum

of 6 to more than 12 pure white 2-inch flowers with greenish throats. Flowers somewhat resemble those of *D. bigibbum* in form.

D. densiflorum. Cool-growing. The 15-inch plants have three to five 6-inch leathery leaves near the top. Drooping 10-inch inflorescences may have fifty to one hundred 2-inch bright yellow flowers with hairy, orange yellow lips in spring or summer.

D. draconis. Cool-growing. The canes are 12 to 18 inches tall, with short, black hairs at their joints. The leaves are 4 inches long, and the 2- to 3-inch fragrant flowers are ivory white with orange or red markings. Early spring bloom.

D. falcorostrum. BEECH ORCHID. Cool-growing. Native to Australia, its 4- to 20-inch pseudobulbs bear two to five 6-inch leathery leaves at their tops. The 4- to 6-inch inflorescences bear up to twenty 1-inch, white, strongly fragrant flowers.

D. farmeri. Cool-growing. This species resembles *D. chrysotoxum*, but its flowers are white or palest lilac with yellow lips.

D. finisterrae. Warm-growing. Canes 2½ feet long bear two leaves at the top. Clusters contain eight to ten 2½-inch flowers, which do not open fully. They are yellowish white spotted with dark red. Bloom may occur in any season.

D. formosum. Warm-growing. The canelike pseudobulbs are 18 inches tall, with 5-inch leathery leaves in the upper portion. Clusters of three to five long-lasting pure white flowers with yellow lips arch outward from the upper stems.

D. gouldii. Warm-growing. Canelike pseudobulbs grow to 4 feet or more. These evergreen plants produce many erect 2-foot sprays of slender white or yellow "antelope horn" flowers with purple-veined lips in late spring and summer.

D. heterocarpum. Warm-growing. Yellowish canes range from 6 inches to 5 feet in length and are clad with many 4- to 5-inch leaves that usually drop off at the end of the growth season. Short spikes bearing two to six flowers may appear at any time of year. The flowers are up to 3 inches across and white to yellow, with a yellowish brown lip marked by red or brown veins.

D. infundibulum. Cool-growing. Slender stems grow 1 to 3 feet in height, with 3- to 5-inch leaves that form all along the stems; all except the topmost leaves drop in autumn. Inflorescences appear at the top of the previous year's growth, lower down on older growths. Each spike bears three to five flowers; these are 3 to 4 inches wide and pure white, with a large, golden yellow blotch on the lip. Spring bloom.

D. johnsoniae. Warm-growing. Slender, canelike pseudobulbs grow 5 to 12 inches tall and have two to five leaves 3 to 6 inches long. Flower spikes 3 to 8 inches tall arise from near the tops of leafy or leafless stems. White flowers 2½ to 5 inches across have wavy edges, and the white lip has a pattern of purple lines in its throat. Fall and winter bloom.

D. kingianum. Cool-growing. A highly variable species, this Australian has tightly clustered stems that may extend 2 inches or 20, thickened at the base and tapering to the leafy top. The flower clusters bear from a few to as many as 20 fragrant, inch-wide (or less) pink flowers. White, red, and bicolored flowers are seen, and many named forms exist. Late winter to early spring bloom. This species thrives out-of-doors where frosts are rare and summer temperatures mild.

D. loddigesii. Cool-growing. Slender stems 4 to 6 inches long sprawl or droop. The fleshy leaves are 1 to 2½ inches long. Single flowers appearing at the joints of leafless stems are 2 inches wide and purple, with a purple-edged orange lip. Spring and summer bloom.

Dendrobium formosum

Dendrobium kingianum

Dendrobium nobile

D. moniliforme. Cool-growing. Slender canes to 16 inches tall produce fragrant flowers singly or in pairs from leafless stems formed the previous year. Flowers are 1 to 2 inches across, white tinged with pink toward the center, with a yellowish green, brown-spotted lip. This Japanese species is hardy outdoors in frost-free regions. A Japanese tradition asserts that the possessor of this plant will enjoy a long life.

D. nobile. Cool-growing. Erect canes grow 12 to 20 inches tall, with two ranks of leaves 2 to 3½ inches long. The leaves last for 2 years. Short inflorescences from both leafy and leafless canes hold two to four fragrant, long-lasting 2½-inch flowers. These may be white to purplish pink, with a yellow or white zone surrounding a large maroon or purple blotch on the lip. Many named varieties and hybrids extend the color range to pure white, pink, purple, red, orange, and yellow. Winter or spring bloom.

D. pierardii. See DENDROBIUM APHYLLUM, page 76.

D. speciosum. ROCK ORCHID. Cool-growing. Native to eastern Australia, where it forms large masses on rocks or trees. The pseudobulbs range in length from 4 to 36 inches, with leathery leaves from 1½ to 10 inches long at the top. Inflorescences 2 to 2½ feet long resemble bushy foxes' tails; they are crowded with 1- to 2-inch feathery white, cream, or yellow flowers with narrow segments. The pleasantly scented flowers appear in winter and spring. This species thrives out-of-doors, on trees or in pots, in California's frost-free coastal belt and similar climates.

D. spectabile. Warm-growing. Pseudobulbs swollen at the base grow as much as 16 inches in length, with fleshy 8- to 9-inch leaves at or near the top. An inflorescence 8 to 16 inches long bears several oddly twisted and curled flowers of cream or yellow, speckled heavily with maroon.

D. thyrsiflorum. Cool-growing. This resembles *D. densiflorum*, but has white or cream-colored flowers with golden yellow lips.

D. trigonopus. Warm-growing. Ten-inch evergreen plants have a few 4-inch leaves at the top. The inflorescences carry one or two 2-inch golden yellow flowers with a green-centered lip. Spring bloom.

D. unicum. Cool-growing. Thin canes grow 6 inches tall, with one to five 2½-inch leaves at the top. The flower clusters are short and carry one to four bright red to orange flowers in autumn and early summer. The flowers are 1½ to 2½ inches wide.

D. victoriae. Cool-growing. The pseudobulbs are 10 inches to 2 feet long and drooping, with leaves 1½ to 3½ inches long at the ends of the stems. When these leaves fall, old stems produce short clusters of small, star-shaped, blue and white flowers. Leafless canes produce flowers for many years. Nearly everblooming.

Dendrobium speciosum 'Clay' CCM/AOS

THE ONCIDIUM ALLIANCE

Dancing dolls, spiders, pansies, tigers—these orchids' common names suggest the wide variety of flower forms to be found in this alliance of 60 or so genera. The "or so" is used advisedly; many of the older genera have been split, creating new names for the orchid lover to master. Moreover, members of the clan are incredibly promiscuous, and the hybrid genera, some of which number as many as six other genera in their ancestry, have become prominent in catalogs and on sales tables. Descriptions of the best-known natural genera are given here first, with the intergeneric hybrids following.

Brassia

BRASSIA

The aptly named spider orchids have long, narrow petals and sepals. Native to tropical America, they can be grown under the same conditions as cattleyas, and appreciate lots of light. The flowers dispose themselves neatly along arching or drooping clusters. Grow them for their form; the colors are muted and the fragrance odd, if perceptible at all. They have contributed something of their long-legged look to a number of intergeneric hybrids.

Brassia arcuigera (B. longissima). The inflorescence can reach 2½ feet, with a half dozen or more yellow or greenish yellow flowers heavily banded with brown. Each flower segment can reach 10 inches in length.

B. caudata. This species resembles *B. arcuigera*, but the flowers are somewhat smaller—to 7 or 8 inches in spread.

B. gireoudiana. The flowers are 10 to 12 inches across with extremely narrow, stiff segments.

B. verrucosa. The spidery flowers are yellowish to lime green with dark red spots and green warts. Their fragrance is musky.

COCHLIODA

These attractive orchids are similar to *Odontoglossum* in habit and require the same cool growing conditions. They have proved extremely important in bringing bright color into a number of hybrids with *Odontoglossum* and *Miltonia*.

Cochlioda noezliana. The 16- to 18-inch inflorescence carries a dozen or more 2-inch, bright reddish orange flowers with a yellow spot on the lip. Summer bloom.

C. rosea. This species resembles *C. noezliana*, but its slightly larger flowers vary from deep rose pink to dark red. Blooms in spring and summer.

Oncidium Sharry Baby

Cuitlauzina pendula

CUITLAUZINA PENDULA

Formerly known as *Odontoglossum pendulum (O. citrosmum)*, this cool grower has 6-inch pseudobulbs and 12-inch leaves. The arching then drooping inflorescence is 1½ to 3 feet long and is crowded with 3-inch pure white or pink-lipped flowers. These appear from late spring to autumn and have a sweet lemony scent.

Grow this orchid in a hanging basket or pot to accommodate the trailing inflorescence. Keep it dry in winter, misting or watering just enough to keep the pseudobulbs from shriveling. It is hardy, possibly to 20°F (−7°C).

LEMBOGLOSSUM

Many of the Mexican and Central American members of *Odontoglossum* have been reassigned to this genus. (It is a reminder of the evanescence of botanical standing that they may eventually be called *Rhynchostele.*) Like members of *Odontoglossum,* they are cool growers, though more warmth tolerant.

Lemboglossum bictoniense (Odontoglossum bictoniense). Foliage clumps to 16 inches produce stiffly erect flowering stems with a host of 2-inch yellow and brown flowers with white or pink lips. Fall blooming.

L. cervantesii. The 6-inch-tall plant produces drooping clusters of two to six 2- to 3-inch white or pale pink flowers. The bases of the petals and sepals are marked by brownish lines that form a series of concentric half-circles. This cool grower has overwintered in the Pacific Coast fog belt with minimal protection.

L. rossii (Odontoglossum rossii). The 8-inch inflorescence bears three to five 2- to 3-inch white, yellow, or pale pink flowers with dark brown spots and stripes. Winter bloom.

L. uro-skinneri (Odontoglossum uro-skinneri). Inflorescences to 2½ feet bear up to twenty 1-inch-wide, green and brown flowers with pink, white-spotted lips.

Lemboglossum cervantesii

MILTONIA, MILTONIOPSIS

These two genera illustrate one of the difficulties that beset orchid nomenclature. Originally they were considered to be one genus, *Miltonia,* with representatives in Colombia and Brazil. The cool-growing Colombian species (native from Costa Rica to Colombia and Ecuador) were extensively grown, hybridized, and improved as "pansy" orchids. Their popularity continues to this day. The Brazilian miltonias, intermediate growers with oncidiumlike flowers, have never been as widely grown. Nevertheless they are, by botanical standards, the true miltonias. The pansy orchids, widely known as miltonias (and called *Miltonia* here), must take botanical second-class status as *Miltoniopsis.*

The pansy orchids produce arching sprays of flat-faced, rounded 4-inch flowers in colors ranging from white to deepest red, usually with contrasting markings. Two common markings are the mask (a solid patch or two large "eyes" of contrasting color) and the waterfall (lines radiating outward and downward from the center of the flower and trailing off into a series of dots).

Miltonia 'Vulcan'

Pansy orchids like the same moderate light as do paphiopedilums (see pages 88–89), and also grow well with phalaenopsis. They require cool nights to flower; night temperatures between 55° and 60°F (13° and 16°C) are ideal. Daytime temperatures are best kept at 80°F (27°C) or less, although brief rises to 90°F (32°C) are tolerated if shading is adequate and humidity high.

Keep plants moist throughout their growing period; withhold water only during dull, gray winter days. Plants bloom best when pot-bound. When repotting becomes necessary, use fine bark with or without perlite. Fertilize monthly, but withhold fertilizer in winter.

Miltoniopsis phalaenopsis. Colombian. Clumps of 8- to 9-inch gray green leaves produce sprays of three to five flowers 2½ to 3 inches wide; these are pure white with purplish red or purple markings on the lip. This is an important parent of the pansy orchids. Late summer and fall bloom.

Miltonia regnellii. Brazilian. The 16-inch flower stalk bears three to five 3-inch flowers of creamy white and pink, with purplish markings. Late summer and fall bloom.

Miltoniopsis roezlii. Colombian. Pale green foliage masses produce two to four 4-inch white flowers with a deep purple blotch. An important parent of the pansy orchids. Winter and spring bloom.

Miltonia spectabilis. Brazilian. The flowers are borne singly on 10-inch stalks; they are white, tinged rose toward the base, and have a purplish red lip. The variety *M. s. moreliana* has larger flowers of dark purple. Autumn bloom.

Miltoniopsis vexillaria. Colombian. Pale green foliage clumps have leaves to 10 inches long. Sprays hold four to six 4-inch flowers of bright rose, marked at the center with white, yellow, and red. Each new growth may produce several sprays. This is a principal parent of many pansy orchids. Spring and summer bloom.

Miltonia 'Memories'

ODONTOGLOSSUM

This once-large genus has been reduced by attrition, all of its Central American and Mexican species having been spirited off into other genera. (Indeed, some botanists think that there is no true distinction between this genus and *Oncidium*.) To avoid confusion those refugees are listed here, but with a cross-reference to their new names. Most of the remaining "true" odontoglossums are cool-growing plants from the high, cool, misty mountains of South America. Many of the hybrids with other genera are more tolerant of intermediate temperatures.

Odontoglossum bictoniense. See LEMBOGLOSSUM BICTONIENSE, page 80.

O. convallarioides. See OSMOGLOSSUM CONVALLARIOIDES, page 84.

O. crispum. Considered by many to be the most beautiful orchid of all, it is also one of the most difficult to grow—unless you live in a cool marine climate. The California

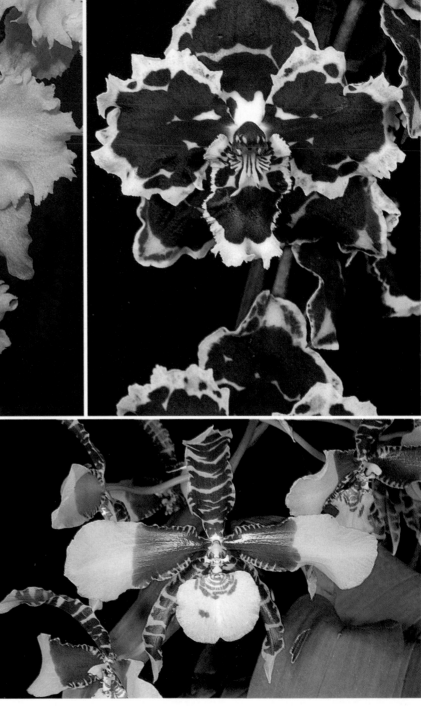

TOP LEFT: *Odontoglossum crispum*
'Colossus'
TOP RIGHT: × *Odontioda* Castle de Ux
'Blackberry' HCC/AOS
BOTTOM RIGHT: *Rossioglossum grande*
'Otani' AM/AOS

fog belt does well with it, as does the Pacific Northwest. Elsewhere, high daytime temperatures will enfeeble and destroy it, unless air-conditioning is available. The 2½- to 3-inch flowers are white or pale rose with fringed and crimped edges and a scattering of reddish brown dots. The 20-inch-long, drooping inflorescences carry 6 to 24 flowers; they usually appear in spring and summer, but may appear at any time.

O. grande. See ROSSIOGLOSSUM GRANDE, page 85.

O. harryanum. The erect inflorescence is 20 to 36 inches tall and bears as many as 12 flowers. These are 3 inches wide, with wavy segments of rich reddish brown marked with yellow. The large lip is reddish brown and white. Summer bloom.

O. luteopurpureum. Like *O. harryanum*, this species carries up to a dozen 3- to 4-inch flowers of chestnut brown marked with yellow. The lip is yellowish white marked with brown. Spring bloom.

O. pendulum. See CUITLAUZINA PENDULA, page 80.

O. pulchellum. See OSMOGLOSSUM PULCHELLUM, page 84.

O. rossii. See LEMBOGLOSSUM ROSSII, page 80.

O. uro-skinneri. See LEMBOGLOSSUM URO-SKINNERI, page 80.

ONCIDIUM

The number of species in *Oncidium* ranges in estimate from 300 to as many as 600. They grow from Mexico and the Caribbean islands to the southern borders of Brazil; a few stragglers have been found in southern Florida. Some grow in the sweltering lowlands; others favor the high, cool, misty mountains. Most will thrive in intermediate temperatures given bright light, ample water during growth and bloom, no complete drying-out, and good air circulation.

Grow oncidiums in pots or baskets filled with bark or perlite and bark. Some of the smaller ones are attractive mounted on pieces of wood, bark, or tree fern. Those with drooping sprays should be grown in hanging baskets. Some have tall, branching inflorescences that will require staking.

In most species slender, branching sprays of flowers come in shades of yellow and red or reddish brown, but a few are white or pink. The flowers of most have flaring petals, often expanded toward the tips, and a full, ruffled lip; to some they suggest dancing dolls or ballerinas. (An earthier imagination might liken them to excitable, full-skirted cheerleaders waving pompoms.) The flowers last well, both on the plant and when cut. Florists call them spray orchids. Only a representative few can be mentioned here.

Oncidium ornithorhynchum

Oncidium ampliatum. Flat, ridged, turtle-shaped pseudobulbs produce leaves to 16 inches long. The branching flower clusters can reach 3 feet and hold hundreds of inch-wide yellow flowers spotted with reddish brown. Spring bloom.

O. carthagenense. A "mule ear" oncidium, in which the fleshy leaves serve the function of pseudobulbs. These nearly erect leaves are up to 20 inches long, and the branching 5- to 6-foot flower stem produces a host of round, ruffled white flowers heavily marked with purplish brown. Summer bloom.

O. cheirophorum. Inch-wide pseudobulbs carry two 4- to 10-inch leaves. The 8-inch flower stem holds many fragrant, firm-textured, bright yellow flowers ½ inch wide. The plant's small size makes it a natural for growing under artificial light. Blooms two or three times a year. This is a fine orchid for beginners.

O. crispum. Moderate-size plants with 8-inch leaves produce flower stems 1½ to 3 feet tall with forty to eighty 3- to 4-inch flowers. These are brown, with ruffled yellow edges and spots of yellow. The large lip has a yellow center. Long-lasting bloom begins in the fall.

O. guianense (O. desertorum). This is one of the equitant oncidiums—those that lack pseudobulbs and display their leaves in fans, somewhat like a miniature iris. The leaf fan is just 1½ inches tall, and the 6-inch flower stem bears several 1-inch, bright yellow flowers. This is a good plant to mount on a branch or on a piece of bark. Fall blooming.

O. kramerianum. See PSYCHOPSIS KRAMERIANA, page 85.

O. lanceanum. Another "mule ear," this striking plant has stiff, erect, brown-mottled leaves 20 inches long and 4 inches wide. The foot-tall flower stem produces a few to several 2- to 2½-inch yellow flowers with heavy reddish brown spotting and a purplish rose lip. Summer blooming.

O. ornithorhynchum. MAIDENHAIR ORCHID. This small species has foot-long leaves and an 18- to 20-inch arching inflorescence crowded with fragrant pink to rosy lilac inch-wide flowers. It appreciates somewhat cool conditions. Summer bloom.

O. papilio. See PSYCHOPSIS PAPILIO, page 85.

O. pusillum. See PSYGMORCHIS PUSILLA, page 85.

O. Sharry Baby. This summer and fall-blooming hybrid produces tall, branching spikes with dozens of 1-inch pinkish or reddish flowers exuding a powerful scent of chocolate (according to some) or vanilla. 'Sweet Fragrance' is a choice selection.

O. sphacelatum. Large pseudobulbs produce narrow leaves up to 3 feet long. Branched inflorescences are 3 to 5 feet tall, erect, and bear scores of inch-wide yellow flowers spotted with reddish brown. Winter to spring bloom.

O. varicosum. Leaves 10 inches long rise above 5-inch pseudobulbs. The arching then drooping inflorescence carries 100 or more 2-inch "dancing doll" flowers in yellow, sparingly marked with red. Winter to spring bloom.

OSMOGLOSSUM

Once included in *Odontoglossum,* these plants differ in having small, white, very fragrant flowers. Less dependent on coolness than *Odontoglossum,* they thrive at intermediate temperatures.

Osmoglossum convallarioides (Odontoglossum convallariodes). A medium-size plant with an inflorescence up to 16 inches long, carrying a few 1-inch white flowers. Spring blooming.

O. pulchellum (Odontoylossum pulchellum). LILY-OF-THE-VALLEY ORCHID. The 20-inch erect or nodding inflorescence bears three to ten creamy flowers 1 to 2 inches across. Their fragrance recalls that of lily-of-the-valley. Spring blooming.

Oncidium lanceanum

PSYCHOPSIS

The butterfly orchids were formerly included in the *Oncidium* genus; they differ from it in producing a succession of single flowers from the top of the inflorescence down. The flowers are large and oddly formed: the dorsal sepal and petals (the upper half of the flower) are extremely narrow, resembling antennae. The lower sepals and lip, in contrast, are broad and strongly marked.

Grow them on a raft or in a pot filled with coarse bark. They prefer intermediate temperatures. Do not remove the flower stalk after the flower fades; it may continue to produce flowers for several years. Bloom is sporadic throughout the year.

Psychopsis papilio

Psychopsis krameriana (Oncidium kramerianum). The flowering stem is 2 to 3 feet tall and carries one single 4- to 5-inch flower at a time. The flower is reddish brown strongly marked with yellow; its lip is yellow with a reddish brown border.

P. papilio (Oncidum papilio). This species strongly resembles *P. krameriana,* but its colors are strongly banded instead of being marked at random.

PSYGMORCHIS PUSILLA

This tiny orchid has no pseudobulbs; instead, its leaves grow in a fan like a miniature iris. The entire plant is just 3 inches tall. Each flowering stem produces one to six 1-inch-wide flowers in succession. These are yellow, with faint brown markings. Grow this one on a bark raft or a piece of tree fern. It needs a humid atmosphere, but the roots should dry out between waterings.

RODRIGUEZIA

These small, easily grown plants come from the forests of Central America and northern South America. Grow them like cattleyas, except that they need no rest period. They flourish either on rafts or potted in fine bark. Give them ample water throughout the year. Bloom may occur at any time of year.

Rodriguezia batemannii. The 10-inch inflorescence, erect or drooping, carries as many as ten fragrant 2½-inch flowers, white marked with yellow or lilac.

R. lanceolata (R. secunda). The 4- to 16-inch inflorescence bears many inch-wide rose red flowers with a white mark at the base of the lip.

R. venusta. White, strongly fragrant flowers 1½ inches wide are borne on a 4- to 8-inch arching inflorescence.

Psygmorchis pusilla

ROSSIOGLOSSUM GRANDE

TIGER ORCHID. This large, very showy orchid thrives in cool to intermediate conditions. The 6- to 12-inch inflorescence carries two to eight 6-inch, glossy, heavy-textured flowers of yellow barred in a deep reddish brown. The growing medium should be fine bark

Rossioglossum grande
'Chestnut Clown' HCC/AOS

containing some leaf mold. Water the plants heavily when in growth; then withhold water, giving them only enough to prevent the shriveling of the pseudobulbs. Repot the plants and resume watering when new growth be-gins. Bloom occurs in winter.

TRICHOCENTRUM

These small growers have relatively large flowers. Their pseudobulbs are small or absent, their leaves fleshy or leathery, their horizontal inflorescences short with few flowers. Grow them on rafts or in pots. They thrive under cattleya conditions.

Trichocentrum albococcineum. The 3-inch inflorescence bears one to three 2-inch flowers of yellow brown or yellow green with a white and purple lip. Late summer to autumn bloom.

T. pulchrum. Similar to *T. albococcineum*, but with white flowers spotted in purplish red.

TRICHOPILIA

These compact, intermediate-temperature orchids have relatively large cattleya-shaped flowers on short, few-flowered stems, several of which may spring from a single pseudobulb. Give plants *Oncidium* conditions: plenty of water during the growing season followed by a 2- to 3-week rest period.

Trichopilia suavis. The short, arching or drooping inflorescence bears from one to four 4-inch flowers. The wavy sepals and petals are creamy white, sometimes spotted with red. The large, wavy-edged lip is white, heavily spotted with rosy red. These flowers are strongly fragrant. Spring bloom.

T. tortilis. The narrow, twisted petals and sepals are brownish purple or rosy lavender. The large, nearly round lip is white, spotted with red and brown. Spring or fall bloom.

INTERGENERIC HYBRIDS

Hybridizers have had a field day crossing the many genera in the *Oncidium* alliance. Most hybrids represent a distinct improvement over their parents, in either appearance or ease of culture. The latter is the result of hybrid vigor *(heterosis):* an increase in size or tolerance of varying conditions that results from the combined genes of the two parents.

The number of these hybrids is so great that only a cursory mention of them is possible here. *Odontoglossum, Oncidium,* and *Miltonia* have been the principal genera involved, but *Cochlioda* and other genera have been used as well.

The genus *Oncidium* contributes both vigor and a free-blooming habit to many of these crosses, along with a propensity to produce yellow and brown flowers with prominent lips. *Miltonia* and *Odontoglossum* contribute large flower size. (The broad petals and sepals of *Odontoglossum* tend to compensate for the small flower parts of *Oncidium*.)

The color range draws on *Oncidium* and *Odontoglossum* for russet and yellow tones. From *Miltonia* comes a velvety finish and broad, rounded contours. *Cochlioda, Rodriguezia,* and *Trichocentrum* contribute bright color and moderate plant size. Crosses involving *Brassia* show a marked increase in the length of the sepals and petals. Following are a few of the many names you are likely to encounter.

× **Aliceara.** Crosses among *Brassia, Miltonia,* and *Oncidium,* these may be either pink or yellow and brown on long sprays.

× **Burrageara.** The ancestry of these hybrids includes *Miltonia, Cochlioda, Odontoglossum,* and *Oncidium*. Plants produce tall, many-flowered spikes with nicely spaced flowers in a variety of colors. They prefer cool to intermediate conditions.

× **Maclellanara.** These hybrids involve *Brassia, Odontoglossum,* and *Oncidium*. The grex Pagan Lovesong has erect spikes to 3 feet bearing many large, star-shaped yellow flowers spotted with brown. The lip is white with brown markings. It prefers cool to intermediate temperatures.

× **Odontioda.** These crosses between *Odontoglossum* and *Cochlioda* yield large, round flowers of *Odontoglossum crispum* form and bright red or brownish red markings profusely scattered over a white or yellow ground. Though cool growers, they tolerate more warmth than does *Odontoglossum*.

× **Odontocidium.** Crosses between *Odontoglossum* and *Oncidium,* these have branched or unbranched inflorescences with yellow, orange, red, or spotted flowers. They are cool to intermediate growers.

× **Odontonia.** Hybrids between *Odontoglossum* and *Miltonia,* these are generally cool growing. Flowers on tall, usually unbranched, stalks are white, yellow, or red, often heavily marked with a contrasting color.

× **Vuylstekeara.** The offspring of × *Odontioda* crossed with *Miltonia,* these have branched or unbranched inflorescences carrying pink, red, or red and white flowers.

× **Wilsonara.** These hybrids number *Cochlioda, Odontoglossum,* and *Oncidium* in their ancestry. Frilly flowers heavily marked in brilliant colors on tall spikes have an *Oncidium* form. These are cool to intermediate growers.

ABOVE: × *Burrageara* Living Fire 'Rustic Red' HCC/AOS
TOP LEFT: × *Wilsonara* Hilda Plumtree 'Glowing Sunset' HCC/AOS
BOTTOM LEFT: × *Odontonia* Danilo 'Golden Gate'

Paphiopedilum insigne
'Harefield Hall' AM/AOS

THE SLIPPER ORCHIDS

These most primitive of orchids stir different emotions in people. The suspicious tend to regard them as threatening, possibly even carnivorous. The orchid lover finds their high gloss and wonderfully subtle coloration endlessly fascinating.

The slipper orchids are not likely to be confused with any others; with the exception of a single species, all the members of the subfamily *Cypripedioideae* have the lip or labellum modified into a pouch, an inflated bag-shaped organ. If you can imagine a dainty foot nestled in this pouch, you'll comprehend these orchids' charming familiar designation as "lady's slippers."

The highly pragmatic purpose of the pouch, however, is to lure an insect, entrap it, and force it to leave the flower with a load of pollen. The uppermost sepal (the *dorsal*) is enlarged and conspicuous. The other two sepals are fused and are called a *synsepalum;* located at the bottom of the flower, the synsepalum is often hidden by the pouch. Two of the petals extend laterally and the third is the pouch.

The flowers are generally waxy and thick textured, lasting well both on the plant and when cut. The leaves are strap shaped and either plain green or mottled (tessellated). They arise as fan-shaped growths from the rhizome and live for many years, though they flower only once. Old plants can have many growths and produce many flowers. The flower stalks emerge from the center of the new growths; those most commonly grown bear a single flower, though some species bear more.

Cypripedium, Paphiopedilum, Phragmipedium, and *Selenipedium* are the four genera in the subfamily. Of these, *Selenipedium* is of little horticultural interest; the plants are large and the flowers generally insignificant. Cold-winter-climate orchid fanciers and wildflower enthusiasts alike would like to grow cypripediums, but they are difficult both to propagate and to grow. (See "Hardy Orchids," pages 47–51.)

Paphiopedilum is a favorite of orchid fanciers. At one time all the slipper orchids were called *Cypripedium,* and a slowly diminishing group of fanciers continues to call the paphiopedilums *Cypripedium,* or cyps (pronounced sips) for short. The more up-to-date call them paphs.

All of these are Old World orchids, native from the Himalayas to Taiwan and eastward to New Guinea and the Solomon Islands. Most cultivated slipper orchids belong to this genus. The tropical New World slipper orchids in *Phragmipedium* are less widely grown, but interest in that genus is increasing.

Most slipper orchids thrive given nighttime temperatures of 60° to 65°F (16° to 18°C), considered an intermediate range for paphiopedilums. The warm-growing slipper orchids require nighttime temperatures of 65° to 70°F (18° to 21°C); some cool growers prefer 55° to 60°F (13° to 16°C). Daytime temperatures should be around 20°F (11°C) warmer. If daytime temperatures exceed 90°F (32°C), provide shade as well as increased humidity.

Paphiopedilum Julius 'San Luis'

All of these orchids are shade lovers, but they differ in the degree of shade preferred. Most thrive given about 1,000 foot-candles of light (see page 20). These preferences and their low stature make them favorites for growing indoors, either at windows or under artificial lights.

PAPHIOPEDILUM

Paphiopedilums grow in a range from sea level (sometimes even within reach of salt spray) to high, cool, moist mountains. Some make their home on trees, but most are terrestrial, growing in moss and leaf mold on rocks or on banks where seepage keeps them supplied with moisture.

Because they lack pseudobulbs in which to store moisture, their roots must never go completely dry. They also require air around their roots, so the planting mix should be porous. Commercial mixes are available, but fine- or medium-grade fir bark mixed with perlite and peat may be used. Hard water containing calcium carbonate is not harmful, but water containing sodium and other salts can be fatal. (Your local water company can advise you on the mineral content of your water.) Never water late in the day; water standing in the fans at night encourages decay.

Paphiopedilum charlesworthii 'Sunside' HCC/AOS

These slipper orchids need repotting every 2 or 3 years, as the potting mix breaks down and becomes less porous. Repotting is best done after bloom. Remove the old mix and replace it with moistened new mix, packing it carefully but firmly around the roots. The leaf fan should rest on the surface of the mix. Water only lightly until new growth begins; then resume regular watering. If plants are very large, they may be divided at repotting: cut or break them into divisions of at least three fans each.

Feed with a half-strength solution of liquid fertilizer every week during spring and summer, and every other week during the winter months.

The genus *Paphiopedilum* consists of roughly 70 species, and named selections have been made from many of these. Hundreds of primary crosses (crosses between two species) exist, and the number of complex crosses (those with three or more species in their ancestry) is legion.

Keep in mind when buying a slipper orchid that plants are sold either as divisions or as seedlings. Divisions of mature plants will exactly resemble the parent, whereas seedlings will resemble it more or less. (Even seedlings

Paphiopedilum bellatulum 'Burmese Bell' AM/AOS

of species show variation.) The few species and hybrid types it is possible to describe here favor intermediate temperatures and light, unless otherwise noted.

Paphiopedilum argus. The leaves are tessellated, and the 12- to 18-inch scape carries a single 5-inch flower. The white dorsal has green stripes and purple spots. Wavy-edged petals are white blushed with pink, veined in green, and lavishly sprinkled with blackish purple spots. The pouch is green and brown. It blooms midwinter to spring.

P. armeniacum. A rambling rhizome produces well-spaced clumps of boldly mottled 4-inch leaves. The 9- to 10-inch flower stalk bears a single pale to bright yellow

4-inch flower with a small dorsal sepal and a large lip with faint red markings near the mouth. It grows best in intermediate to warm conditions. Grow it in a basket of slats or wire mesh to accommodate the running rhizome. Spring or summer bloom.

P. barbatum. Clumps of tessellated leaves produce 12- to 14-inch stalks bearing one or two 4-inch flowers. The large dorsal is white, with green and purple stripes. Slightly drooping maroon petals have blackish purple warts. The pouch is purple. Blooms in early winter, sometimes reblooming in spring.

P. bellatulum. This dwarfish plant has strongly mottled leaves and a flower stalk that holds the nearly round flower just 1½ to 3 inches above the foliage. The flower is white, finely sprinkled with spots and blotches of maroon; its small pouch is the same color. The dorsal sepal and petals are nearly round. This intermediate to warm grower likes both night temperatures and brightness in the higher ranges and needs excellent drainage. A midwinter rest, with slightly less water and at slightly lower temperatures, will induce summer to fall bloom. *Paphiopedilum concolor, P. godefroyae,* and *P. niveum* are all similar in appearance and requirements.

Paphiopedilum venustum

P. callosum. Resembles *P. barbatum,* but with more intense pinkish tones in the petals and pouch. Blooms early spring through autumn.

P. charlesworthii. The 4-inch flower rises above the green foliage clump on a 6-inch stalk. The very large dorsal sepal is pink, with deeper pink veining and a narrow white rim. The smaller petals and pouch are brownish flushed with pink. Autumn bloom.

P. delenatii. Dark green 4-inch leaves are marked above with paler green and below with purple. The clumps are spaced out along a rambling rhizome. The 9-inch flower stalk produces one and sometimes two 4-inch pale pink to white flowers with a pink pouch. This species blooms in spring.

P. druryi. Long rhizomes produce scattered clumps of 6- to 18-inch light green leaves and 10-inch flower stalks bearing a single, nearly 4-inch, yellow to greenish flower with a bold purple stripe on each petal and on the dorsal sepal. This intermediate grower blooms in late winter and early spring and likes strong, indirect light and warm days coupled with cool nights.

P. fairrieanum. The leaves are green, sometimes faintly tessellated. The 5- to 18-inch flower stalk bears a single flower 4 inches tall and somewhat narrower. The tall dorsal sepal has frilled edges and is white, heavily marked with green and purple stripes. The similarly colored petals droop for two-thirds of their length, then turn sharply upward, giving the flower a somewhat whimsical aspect. Colors can vary from white and green to white and deep purple. An intermediate to cool grower, it blooms in late fall and early winter.

P. haynaldianum. Yellowish green, large leaves surround flower stems that can reach 20 inches and carry two to four 5-inch flowers. The dorsal sepal is narrow at the base and white with purple stripes in the lower half; it has a sprinkling of maroon spots. The narrow, widely spreading petals are yellowish green heavily marked with maroon spots near the base. The large pouch is greenish tan with dark green veins. Bloom occurs in late winter and spring.

P. henryanum. The leaves are somewhat more than 6 inches long, plain green with some purple suffusion underneath. The 6-inch flower stem carries a single 3-inch flower having a yellow dorsal heavily marked in dark purple with deep pink petals and lip. This species blooms in winter to early spring.

P. insigne. This widely grown and variable species has plain green leaves and a 9-inch stalk bearing a single 5-inch flower. The dorsal sepal is yellowish green or pale green with a white edge and raised spots of purple or brown. The narrow petals are yellowish green to yellowish brown. The flower has a high gloss. Plants are hardy to almost 32°F (0°C) but intolerant of protracted warmth. Bloom period is fall and early winter.

P. javanicum. The leaves are sparingly tessellated, and flower stalks 6 to 14 inches tall carry a single 4-inch flower. Its dorsal sepal is narrow and greenish white, striped green and with a sharp white tip. Narrow, spreading petals are green with purple tips. Bloom season is irregular, but usually in summer.

P. malipoense. The 4- to 8-inch leaves are boldly mottled. The 10-inch flower stalk carries a single 3-inch flower whose dorsal sepal and petals are green marked with faint purple lines. The large, baggy pouch is somewhat translucent and stained pink by profuse maroon dotting inside. A warm grower, it blooms in fall and winter. Grow it in a basket of slats or wire mesh to accommodate the running rhizome.

P. micranthum. As in *P. armeniacum,* the foliage clumps are spaced along a wandering rhizome. The leaves are 2 to 6 inches long and dark green mottled in lighter green. The 3- to 8-inch flower stalk carries a single 3-inch-wide flower with a short, nearly round dorsal and petals of greenish yellow marked with purplish pink lines. The very large, puffy lip is 3 inches long and pink. This is an intermediate to warm grower.

P. spiceranum. Clumps of green leaves produce 10-inch arching flower stalks that carry a single 3-inch flower. The large white dorsal sepal is narrow at the base, then spreads upward and folds back to emulate a small calla *(Zantedeschia).* A maroon vertical streak decorates the front. Petals are yellowish green suffused with brown, and the margins near the flower center are deeply crimped. This intermediate to cool grower blooms in autumn and early winter.

P. sukhakulii. Clumps of tessellated leaves produce 10-inch stems bearing a single 5-inch flower. The dorsal sepal is white with a fine striping of green. The horizontally spreading petals are green, heavily spotted with blackish purple. Bloom is in autumn, sometimes also in spring. This species has been a parent to many fine hybrids.

P. superbiens. The 6- to 10-inch leaves are strongly mottled. The 6- to 10-inch flower stalk carries a single 5-inch flower with a broad, sharply pointed dorsal of white flushed pink and heavily streaked with green and purple veins. Long, narrow, downwardly angled petals shade from green at the base to purple toward the tips. The glossy lip is dark maroon and 2½ inches long. This intermediate grower blooms in summer.

P. venustum. Heavily tessellated leaf clumps give rise to 5- to 10-inch flower stalks carrying a single 5-inch flower. The low, broad sepal is white, heavily striped in dark green. The petals are greenish white with green veins; their outer third is coppery or purple. The lip is yellow or coppery with strong green veining. Bloom is in winter.

MULTIFLOWERING PAPHIOPEDILUMS

Several species of *Paphiopedilum* have flower stalks that carry from 2 to (rarely) 20 flowers. These typically open sequentially—one fading and falling as the next opens—but some have several flowers open at a time. These are not the easiest plants to grow, and beginners are urged to gain experience before attempting them.

Paphiopedilum glanduliferum (P. praestans). Dark green leaves are 14 to 16 inches long. The 12- to 20-inch flower stalk carries from two to five flowers. The tall, narrow dorsal is 2 inches long and half as wide, yellow with pronounced purple stripes. The lower sepals are similar. Narrow petals angle downward at a 45° angle; they are yellow veined with maroon, and are fringed at the edge. The lip is 2 inches long or more, yellow marked with maroon. It blooms in summer.

P. glaucophyllum. The leaves are 12 to 20 inches long and either green or faintly mottled. The flower stalk can reach 2 feet and produce up to 20 flowers—usually one at a time, rarely two. The flowers have a broad cream to green dorsal heavily spotted and striped with purple. Petals are 1½ to 2 inches long and white, with many deep pink to maroon spots as well as tufts of short hairs along the edges. The lip or pouch is 1½ inches long and pink finely stippled with maroon. The variety *P. g. moquettianum* is slightly larger, and the dorsal is speckled rather than veined. It blooms in summer or at any time and is a warm grower.

Paphiopedilum micranthum

Paphiopedilum sanderianum 'Jacob's Ladder'

P. philippinense. Clumps of dark green 6- to 20-inch leaves produce flowering stems to 20 inches, each bearing two to five flowers. Both the dorsal sepal and the fused lower sepals are 2 inches long, white striped with maroon. Petals are narrow, yellow at the base fading to maroon. They are somewhat drooping, twisted, narrow, and up to 5 inches long. This species blooms in late winter or spring bloom.

P. rothschildianum. This spectacular species is slow to reach blooming age after division and seems to resent transplanting. Its dark green leaves can reach 2 feet in length, and the 18-inch flower stalk carries from two to four flowers with a petal span of up to 10 inches. The 2½-inch-long dorsal sepal is cream, green, or yellow. The long, narrow petals are yellow or cream striped with maroon, the pouch tawny or yellowish suffused with dark red. Bloom is in late spring or early summer.

P. sanderianum. The dark green, straplike leaves are 12 to 18 inches long. The flower stalk is 18 inches tall and carries two to five flowers. The 2½-inch dorsal sepal is yellow, striped in deep maroon. Narrow, twisting, drooping petals are 12 to 36 inches long, yellow at the base with maroon spots and becoming deep maroon in their last three-quarters. This species is rare and expensive.

P. stonei. The leaves can reach 28 inches in length, and the flower stem can reach 28 inches; it bears two to four large flowers. The dorsal sepal is broadly oval, 2 inches tall and wide, and white with a few dark purple vertical lines. The petals arch out and down and are yellow, dotted and flushed in maroon. The lip is creamy or white at the base, deep pink toward the front. It blooms in late summer or early autumn.

P. victoria-mariae. Heavily mottled leaves are 10 to 12 inches long. The flowering spike can reach 3 to 4 feet in height and must be staked. It elongates as flowering progresses, usually one bloom at a time, to a total of 20 blooms or more. Each flower has a 1-inch dorsal of cream or yellow with a green center striped with maroon. The 1½-inch petals are narrow, twisted, and reddish purple; the 1½-inch lip is purple with a whitish or greenish rim. There is a long bloom season beginning in spring or summer.

Paphiopedilum Winston Churchill 'Prime Minister'

Paphiopedilum Maudiae

HYBRID PAPHIOPEDILUMS

You are more likely to encounter hybrids than you are the species paphs. Many are first-generation crosses between two species, but many, many more are complex hybrids—hybrids of hybrids, sometimes involving multiple remote ancestral species. The orchid plant you buy may be a seedling, in which case it will bear a grex name (see page 14). Grexes guarantee only a greater or lesser resemblance to other seedlings from the same cross. On the other hand, if your plant is a division, it will be more expensive but identical to its parent. For instance, you will come across many plants named Winston Churchill, a grex name. But if you see Winston Churchill 'Indomitable', it will be a division of an award-winning plant, not just a relative. In many cases seedlings of a new cross or of a repeated cross are offered. The sales effort here is likely to be based on great expectations: "Expect tall stems carrying full, rounded blooms in shades of pink and green. Could be a winner!" These predictions are based on growers' experiences with similar crosses in the past—or perhaps on their hopes.

New hybrids appear at a frantic pace. During 3 months in a recent year, 80 new hybrid paphs were registered. All tend to be sturdy plants with broad, rounded flowers having clearly defined colors and a high gloss. Here are a few of the countless hybrid grexes.

Paphiopedilum Harrisianum. This, the first hybrid paphiopedilum, dates from 1866. Flowers tend to dark burgundy red, faintly striped with white in the dorsal sepal.

P. Makuli. These flowers have white dorsals striped in green and purple, pale petals spotted with maroon, and russet red pouches.

P. Maudiae. These plants bear tessellated leaves and sturdy stalks holding white flowers with green striping. Later crosses involving darker forms of the original species have yielded plants of similar vigor and striping, but in pink (*coloratum*) and dark red (*vinicolor*) shades.

P. Winston Churchill. Large, well-rounded flowers of heavy texture characterize this grex. Dorsals are big and broad, white, and heavily spotted or flared with deep red.

TROPICAL AMERICAN SLIPPERS

Members of the Central and South American genus *Phragmipedium* have not enjoyed the popularity of *Paphiopedilum,* but interest in them and their hybrids has been rising rapidly since the introduction of the bright red *Phragmipedium besseae.* These plants superficially resemble those of the Asiatic slippers, as do their flowers, but there are significant differences. The flower stem is jointed, has conspicuous bracts, may be branched, and normally bears many flowers. Chromosomal differences between the two make intergeneric crossing very difficult. Although both genera are alike culturally, there is one significant difference: *Phragmipedium* is strongly acid loving, so cannot tolerate lime or hard water.

Phragmipedium besseae. This orchid was discovered only in 1981—rather a marvel, considering its bright color. The dark green foliage clump sends up a bloom stalk that bears from one to six flowers that open in succession. The flowers measure a bit less than 2½ inches wide and 2 inches high. All their segments, including the pouch, are bright red. Recent seedlings and hybrids have shown color variations tending toward orange and yellow.

P. caudatum. Leaves of this spectacular orchid are 2 to 3 feet long. The yard-tall flower stem displays two to four flowers open at one time on individual 6-inch stalks. The dorsal sepal is cream colored, with a netting of maroon to brown or green veins. The long, twisting petals open as much as 6 inches in length and elongate over several days to a possible 36 inches. Petal growth stops if the tips encounter a solid surface, so the plant should be grown in a hanging basket or supported on a pedestal. The petals are initially colored like the dorsal sepal, but toward the tips the color becomes deep rose or purplish red.

P. klotzscheanum. These clashing consonants belong to a slipper orchid with narrow, sedgelike leaves 12 to 15 inches long. The flowering stem is 2 feet tall and produces as many as six flowers in succession. The dorsal sepal is 2 inches tall and pale greenish brown striped with maroon. The drooping 4-inch petals display the same color. The pouch is yellow, with a white interior and a speckling of purple.

P. lindleyanum. The leaves are deep green and 1½ to 2 feet long. The flower spike can be up to a yard tall and bear (one or two at a time) as many as 30 green and rose flowers with yellow or green lips. The overall flower size is somewhat under 3 inches.

P. pearcei. The leaves are deep green and 10 to 18 inches long. The two to four 5-inch flowers are green and white with a suffusion of pink. The lip is just over 1 inch long and is green, often with purple dots at the mouth.

P. sargentianum. The green leaves are yellow edged and up to 1½ feet in length. The tall (possibly 4 feet or more) flower stem carries as many as five flowers, which open in succession and resemble those of *P. lindleyanum.*

P. schlimii. The bright green leaves are up to 1 foot long. The branched 1-foot flower stalk produces from two to six flowers. Petals and sepals are broadly rounded and the lip is broad and puffy. The flowers are pink or white, or a combination of the two, and are 2 inches across.

Many hybrid phragmipediums have been produced: *P.* × Grande, a cross between *P. caudatum* and *P. longifolium,* is notable for the length of its twisted petals. Other hybrids involving *P. besseae* and *P. schlimii* tend to display pink, white, red, or yellow colors.

ABOVE: *Phragmipedium* × Grande
'The Wizard' AM/AOS
BELOW: *Phragmipedium besseae*
'Laurie Susan Weltz' AM/AOS

THE BOTANICALS

After mastering Cattleya, Paphiopedilum, and Phalaenopsis, the budding orchid collector will wish to conquer new worlds. As Publilius Syrus observed, "No pleasure endures unseasoned by variety." The next step is to begin exploring the botanicals, less well known orchids that have not achieved broad commercial success but that nevertheless reward us with their beauty or their uniqueness.

They are called botanicals because, being of little importance to commercial growers and florists, they were once considered interesting solely to botanists. (It is worth noting that keen orchid enthusiasts usually become keen amateur botanists sooner or later.) Some of these botanicals are as strikingly handsome as members of the more familiar genera, but many are grown for their curious form and color or, in some cases, for their grotesqueness. Many, but by no means all, are small enough to fill in the spaces between larger plants in a collection.

Masdevallia ignea 'Blumen Insel'
HCC/AOS

AËRANGIS

Sixty or so species of small to medium monopodial orchids related to *Angraecum* range from Africa to Madagascar and the islands of the Indian Ocean. Their short stems bear two ranks of leathery leaves. Erect to arching or drooping inflorescences carry many white or creamy flowers with long spurs. The flowers of many are fragrant at night. Grow these orchids in small pots filled with bark, or on rafts or logs. They like warm temperatures and medium to low light.

Aërangis biloba. The 8-inch plants have four to ten opposing, 6-inch, leathery, dark green leaves with black dots. The pendent spike is 4 to 16 inches long and bears up to 20 long-spurred white flowers, sometimes faintly tinged with pink. Spring bloom.

A. citrata. This miniature plant is less than 4 inches tall, with 3½-inch leaves. Its many drooping, 10-inch spikes are crowded with tiny white, lemon-scented flowers. Spring bloom.

A. luteoalba rhodosticta. Short-stemmed plants carry two or three 6-inch dark green leaves. Arching or drooping inflorescences to 1 foot long bear up to 24 unscented white or cream flowers with a red column. Spring and fall bloom.

Angraecum × Veitchii

ANGRAECUM

Like *Aërangis* a native to Africa and the islands of the Indian Ocean, most in this genus differ in being large plants. Their flowers are star shaped, with spreading segments and a long spur attached to the lip. The flower color is white, cream, or greenish. Grow these in pots or baskets filled with a coarse mix; water and feed them freely throughout the year, keeping temperatures warm and giving them medium to high light. The plants will develop many aerial roots. Mist frequently, but early enough in the day to keep water from standing in the leaf bases at night.

Angraecum distichum. Unlike most of its genus, this is a small plant with drooping, branching stems closely set with short, overlapping leaves in a braided effect.

Angraecum sesquipedale

The stems can reach 10 inches in length. Small white flowers less than an inch wide appear between the leaves toward the branch ends. The flowers are fragrant at night. May flower in any season.

A. eburneum. Large, erect stems form large clumps of two-ranked leaves that are leathery, deep green, and 12 to 16 inches long. The arching inflorescences are longer than the leaves and hold up to fifteen 2½-inch green flowers with a large white lip. The flowers are fragrant and the lip uppermost, giving the flowers an upside-down look. Winter blooming.

A. sesquipedale. The Latin species name means "foot and a half" and refers to the long spurs (actually only 10 to 12 inches long) on the spicily fragrant 5- to 8-inch white flowers. These are borne in groups of one to four on an inflorescence somewhat shorter than the 10- to 16-inch leaves. The plant can reach 4 feet in height. Winter blooming.

A. × Veitchii. This hybrid between *A. eburneum* and *A. sesquipedale* is similar to the latter in size and carries six to ten 3-inch flowers that open greenish or ivory before turning pure white. Winter blooming.

ANGULOA

TULIP ORCHID. The tulip orchids may be epiphytic, but they are more commonly grown as terrestrials, in a mix suitable for *Cymbidium*. The pseudobulbs are topped by three large (2½-foot by 1-foot), thin, heavily ribbed leaves. The flowers spring from the base of the pseudobulbs, each on its own short, stout stem. The sepals are larger than the petals and cupped around them, lending the flower its tulip shape. Feed and water these cool growers heavily during the summer growth period; provide medium to low light, shading them against sunburn. Then keep them on the dry side, with maximum brightness, until signs of new growth appear. Summer bloom. Crossed with *Lycaste*, tulip orchids form hybrids called × *Angulocaste*, whose flowers are less cupped, more open and triangular than the species.

Anguloa clowesii. The flowers are bright yellow and 3 to 3½ inches wide; they have a fragrance reminisent of chocolate and mint.

A. ruckeri. Flowers are somewhat less cupped than those of *A. clowesii* and are olive or bronze on the outside, heavily spotted with red inside. The flowers of some may be all red or ivory white.

Anguloa clowesii 'Ruth' CCM/AOS

Ansellia africana

ANSELLIA AFRICANA

LEOPARD ORCHID. These warm growers flourish in strong light. Tall (to 3 feet), cane-like pseudobulbs carry up to ten leaves 6 to 20 inches long and produce branching inflorescences with many 2-inch flowers, whose narrow yellow segments are heavily spotted with dark brown. Flowering is in winter. The plants are sometimes sold as *A. gigantea* or *A. nilotica;* those so named may have broader, more brightly colored flowers than the species.

BIFRENARIA

Resembling *Anguloa* and *Lycaste* in form and flower, these orchids have firm, conical pseudobulbs, each topped by a single large, broad, heavily veined, leathery leaf. Short stems from the base of the pseudobulbs carry from one to five firm, waxy flowers that resemble those of cymbidiums. These plants grow best in a coarse bark mixture and bloom best when pot-bound. Give them intermediate to warm temperatures and bright light. Water and feed them freely until growth is completed; then give them cooler, drier conditions until new growth appears.

Bifrenaria harrisoniae. The leaves measure 12 inches by 5 inches, and the inflorescence carries one or two 3-inch, ivory to greenish yellow flowers with a rose to red lip. Some plants have a rosy suffusion, and a rare form is pure white. The spring flowers are highly fragrant.

B. tetragona. These flowers are smaller than those of *B. harrisoniae* and are green, heavily suffused with brown. Summer bloom.

B. tyrianthina. The flowers are somewhat larger than those of *B. harrisoniae* and are pinkish purple in color, paler toward the center. The lip is pinkish purple. Spring blooming.

BLETILLA

See "Hardy Orchids," pages 47–51.

BULBOPHYLLUM (INCLUDING CIRRHOPETALUM)

This enormous genus contains over 1,000 species of highly diverse size, appearance, and nativity. Examples are found on every continent, but most are East Asian or Indonesian. Their general preference is for intermediate to warm temperatures and bright, diffused light.

Some have tightly clustered pseudobulbs, others long, slender rhizomes with widely scattered growths. Some have large and fragrant flowers, others tiny ones that smell like dead animals. Most have a lip that is hinged and movable. The flowers may be large and solitary, or tiny and closely set on fleshy spikes. Some have narrow flowers that radiate outward from the top of the stalk like the ray flowers on a daisy; this last group is sometimes split from its parent genus and named *Cirrhopetalum.*

Bulbophyllum lobbii
Petite Plaisance

Bulbophyllum barbigerum. Tightly clustered, inch-thick, round pseudobulbs produce 4-inch leaves and 8-inch inflorescences with as many as a dozen inch-wide purple, narrow-petaled flowers. Each has a projecting narrow lip tipped with a dense clump of fine red to purple hairs, which flutter in the lightest breeze.

B. graveolens (Cirrhopetalum graveolens). Pseudobulbs 3 inches thick are tipped by 18-inch leaves and a wheel-shaped inflorescence made up of long, narrow, yellowish green flowers with purplish red lips.

B. imbricatum. Grow this one for its oddity, not its beauty. The 5-inch flower stalk is closely covered with dark purplish, scalelike bracts, making it resemble a slender lizard. The minute, dark purple flowers peep out from under the bracts a few at a time. Bloom is, if not striking, at least nearly continuous.

B. lobbii. Clumps of 2-inch pseudobulbs produce single 4-inch flowers on a 6-inch stem. The flower is fragrant, long lasting, yellow striped with brown, and oddly shaped, with a tall dorsal sepal and lateral sepals that sweep outward, downward, and then back toward the stalk. Spring and summer bloom.

B. longiflorum (Cirrhopetalum umbellatum). Clumping pseudobulbs produce 3½-inch leaves and 8-inch inflorescences topped by a half circle of cream to yellow flowers with red spots and a dark red lip. The inflorescence can measure 4 inches across. Fall and winter bloom.

B. macranthum. Inch-long pseudobulbs produce fleshy 10-inch leaves. Solitary flowers are 2½ inches broad, with dark red petals speckled with deeper red and green or yellow sepals. The lip is tiny.

B. medusae (Cirrhopetalum medusae). The inflorescence is a mophead of 5-inch-long, straw-colored sepals that trail like the tentacles of a jellyfish. Fall and winter bloom.

B. ornatissimum (Cirrhopetalum ornatissimum). Two-inch pseudobulbs produce 6-inch leaves. The flower stalk is slightly longer than the leaves and carries three 4-inch yellow flowers marked with purple. The lateral sepals give the flowers their length; other flower parts are small.

Calanthe Takane

CALANTHE

These terrestrial plants are of two different origins and require correspondingly different care. Most tropical kinds are completely deciduous, blooming from the bare pseudobulbs; those native to Japan, on the other hand, are evergreen and have no visible pseudobulbs. Both kinds have erect or arching inflorescences bearing many flowers.

The tropical species have been in cultivation for many years and were popular house plants in Victorian England, but their size and leaflessness while in bloom limit their usefulness in today's smaller houses. The Japanese calanthes have been favorites in Japan for centuries, but they are so far only promising novelties elsewhere. They may be grown out-of-doors, with care, where temperatures rarely dip below freezing.

The tropical, deciduous species need bright light and warmth while their foliage and pseudobulbs are developing. Once the leaves yellow and drop, dry out the plants thoroughly and repot them, discarding any withered pseudobulbs and dead roots. Set the bases of the remaining bulbs in a rich, highly organic mix and raise the heat and humidity until winter flowering ensues. Feed and water heavily to produce large new growth.

In nature the Japanese species are woodland plants that grow in rich soil with leaf mold; in cultivation they are grown in lava rock and fertilized frequently. They are tolerant of cool to warm temperatures.

Calanthe discolor. Japanese. These plants have two to four 6- to 10-inch leaves; inflorescences 8 to 16 inches tall carry up to thirty 2-inch flowers. These may be dark brown to reddish orange, purple, yellow, bright green, or white, with a white or pink lip veined in red or yellow. The spring flowers are fragrant.

C. sieboldii. Japanese. Similar to *C. discolor*, but with 2-foot inflorescences that carry 10 to 16 yellow or yellow green flowers. There are many other Japanese species, as well as a number of named hybrids that may someday reach North America.

C. vestita. Tropical and deciduous. The pseudobulbs are 8 or 9 inches tall, the inflorescences (to 3 feet tall) erect then nodding, carrying a dozen or more long-lasting flowers in winter. These are white with touches of yellow or red on the lip. Pleated leaves 2 feet tall follow. The variety 'Baron Schroeder' has pink flowers, as does the hybrid *C. × Veitchii*.

CATASETUM

The species of *Catasetum* are remarkable in two ways: First, though most orchids contain both male and female parts (and are hence botanically "perfect"), catasetums may produce solely male or solely female flowers—and the sex of the flowers can change with plant stress. Second, male flowers shoot their pollen onto visiting insects by a triggerlike device. A favorite jest of the seasoned orchid fancier is to persuade a novice to smell the flower; when nose touches trigger, it receives the pollen forcibly (but not painfully).

Catasetum pileatum 'Green Giant' AM/AOS

Catasetums are native to the American tropics and are generally plants with large, fleshy pseudobulbs and large, pleated, deciduous leaves. They flourish in intermediate to warm temperatures, but need protection from strong sunlight.

Water and feed them liberally while they are actively growing; withhold water when leaves begin to fall, providing only enough to keep the pseudobulbs from shriveling. Resume watering when new growth appears in the spring. Bloom period is fall and winter.

Catasetum expansum. Arching inflorescences display fragrant white to yellow or green flowers. 'Pireo' is a selection with green flowers heavily spotted in red.

C. fimbriatum. The drooping inflorescence is up to 3 feet long, with many fragrant flowers. The male flowers are 2 inches wide, yellow to green with a pink to red suffusion and maroon streaks. The female flowers are yellowish green.

C. integerrimum. Arching inflorescences to 16 inches carry up to ten hooded, fragrant, green to yellow green flowers with a few brownish red markings.

C. macrocarpum. The foot-long inflorescence is erect or arching and bears up to ten fragrant flowers. These are waxy and yellowish green marked with purplish red; the lip has white markings.

C. pileatum. A drooping inflorescence to 16 inches long carries several flowers. The male flowers are 4 inches wide and creamy white, sometimes tinged with green. The female flowers are ivory with a yellow lip.

C. russellianum. See CLOWESIA RUSSELLIANA, below.

C. tenebrosum. Trailing inflorescences produce many dark purplish red flowers with large, bright yellow lips in spring and summer.

C. viridiflavum. The gracefully arching foot-long inflorescences produce 4-inch fragrant flowers of ivory to pale yellow, with a pale orange interior lip.

C. warscewiczii. See CLOWESIA WARSCEWICZII, below.

CIRRHOPETALUM

See BULBOPHYLLUM, page 96.

CLOWESIA

Members of *Clowesia* resemble *Catasetum*, except that the flowers are (like those of most orchids) "perfect": that is, both male and female.

Clowesia rosea. The 5-inch trailing inflorescences hold several bell-shaped, inch-wide flowers of pale to deep pink. The lip is heavily fringed. Crossing this species with some of the large, flat-flowered catasetums has yielded attractive hybrids.

C. russelliana (Catasetum russellianum). This is similar to *C. rosea*, but with green flowers and a white-edged lip.

C. warscewiczii (Catasetum warscewiczii). The 12-inch drooping inflorescence of this orchid displays green to white flowers.

COELOGYNE

Species of *Coelogyne* are found from the high, cool Himalayas to the steamy jungles of Borneo and eastward. Flower colors range from pure white through orange and brown to green and nearly black. All plants are epiphytic and possess pseudobulbs with leaves that emerge from the top. Some have rambling rhizomes with widely spaced pseudobulbs; these are best grown on long rafts. The inflorescences may be erect or drooping, one or many flowered. In general, they thrive in cool to intermediate temperatures and bright light; exceptions are noted.

Coelogyne cristata

   Coelogyne cristata. From high elevations in the Himalayas, this orchid requires cool growing conditions. (In fact, it can withstand near-freezing temperatures.) Where house or greenhouse summer temperatures are high, the plant may be suspended outside in a shady, breezy location. Fragrant flowers, three to ten per arching 6- to 12-inch inflorescence, are 3 to 4 inches wide and pure white, with yellow markings on the lip. Winter and spring bloom.

   C. dayana. Trailing inflorescences 2 to 3 feet long are set with 20 to 30 cream to pale yellow to pale brown flowers, whose brown lips are marked with white. This Borneo native prefers warm conditions and blooms in spring or summer.

   C. lawrenceana. The flower stem is 6 to 12 inches tall and carries a single 5-inch, greenish yellow to yellow flower. Its large red or white lip is tinged with yellow and marked with brown protuberances. Give it intermediate temperatures and expect spring bloom.

   C. massangeana. See C. TOMENTOSA, below.

   C. nitida (C. ochracea). The erect or nodding 8-inch inflorescence carries from three to six fragrant white flowers with white lips marked red and yellow. Flowers are 1½ inches in width. Summer bloom.

   C. pandurata. Widely spaced pseudobulbs indicate that this plant should be grown on a long raft or in a basket. The 6- to 12-inch inflorescence carries several 4- to 5-inch lime green flowers; their green lips are prominently marked with black. Summer bloom. Warm temperatures.

   C. speciosa. This species is much like *C. lawrenceana,* but with yellowish green to greenish tan flowers having a brown lip. Fall bloom.

   C. tomentosa (C. massangeana). A drooping inflorescence to 18 inches long carries twenty to thirty 2-inch fragrant flowers of pale yellow, ivory, or light brown. Their lips are dark brown marked with yellow. Spring through fall bloom. Warm or cool temperatures.

CYCNOCHES

SWAN ORCHIDS. The 60 or so species of swan orchids are native to tropical America. They are related to *Catasetum* and, like that genus, bear either male or female flowers. The common name springs from the long, arching column of the male flower, which resembles a swan's neck. The male flower is able to throw pollen onto pollenizing bees; the female flower has a shorter column with three

Cycnoches chlorochilon 'Cherimoya' AM/AOS

Dendrochilum cobbianum

hooks that strip the pollen from the bees. The flowers are fragrant. These plants like ample water and feeding while making new growth, followed by a brief rest period with reduced watering. Grow them in intermediate to warm temperatures, but protect them from strong sunlight.

Cycnoches chlorochilon (C. ventricosum chlorochilon). The male inflorescence is 6 to 12 inches long, holding several 5-inch flowers of gray or pale green with white lips. Summer to fall bloom.

C. egertonianum. The male inflorescence is a drooping 16 to 36 inches in length, boasting up to 30 open flowers at one time. Fragrant and long lasting, each flower is 3 inches wide and green or greenish brown with purple markings. It is autumn flowering.

C. loddigesii. A drooping inflorescence 6 to 12 inches long carries a half dozen fragrant, 5-inch, pale green to greenish brown to yellow flowers mottled with reddish brown. The lips are white to pale pink. Fall bloom.

C. ventricosum. This species differs from *C. chlorochilon* in being somewhat smaller in flower and having petals and sepals swept backward.

CYPRIPEDIUM

See "Hardy Orchids," pages 47–51.

CYRTOPODIUM

Large size and muted flower color have kept these plants out of mainstream orchid culture, but one species is noteworthy as the largest orchid native to the United States.

Cyrtopodium punctatum. BEE-SWARM ORCHID. South Florida is home to this giant. Torpedo-shaped pseudobulbs can reach a yard in height. Leaves on the younger pseudobulbs are up to 2 feet long; they are shed during the winter. The inflorescence is stout, branching, and to 5 feet or more in height. The 1½-inch flowers are greenish yellow heavily spotted with brown. Bloom is in spring. Plants can be grown in large pots or mounted on a tree. They like bright light, plenty of water during growth and bloom, and considerable drying-out while dormant.

DACTYLORRHIZA

See "Hardy Orchids," pages 47–51.

DENDROCHILUM

These small orchids are grown for their graceful carriage and delightful perfume. Plants are small, compact, and attractive, their many pseudobulbs topped by one or two leaves. Long arching and trailing spikes are closely set with tiny flowers in a chain or necklace effect. A small pot can contain many flowering growths, creating a fountain of bloom. They do well in intermediate temperatures and bright light.

Dendrochilum cobbianum. The leaves are a foot long. The arching then drooping spikes can reach 20 inches in length and contain dozens of ¾-inch white or greenish white flowers with an orange yellow lip. It can flower in any season.

D. filiforme. Like *D. cobbianum* in size and habit, this species has very slender spikes displaying as many as 100 tiny yellow flowers. Summer and fall bloom.

D. glumaceum. This species resembles *D. cobbianum,* differing in having large bracts among partly closed flowers of white with orange yellow lips. Fall bloom.

D. uncatum. This is a miniature *D. filiforme,* with 4-inch leaves and a 4-inch straw yellow inflorescence. Summer and fall bloom.

D. wenzelii. This species' leaves are 8 inches long by ¼ inch wide. The inflorescence is packed with flowers ³/₈ inch across. Although usually red, these may be yellow, orange, or brown. The bloom season is winter.

Disa uniflora

DISA UNIFLORA

Of the 100-plus species of the terrestrial African orchid genus *Disa,* only *D. uniflora (D. grandiflora)* is seen, and that but seldom. Native to stream banks near Cape Town, it is sometimes known as the "pride of Table Mountain." Plants are 6 inches to 2 feet tall and bear one to three (rarely more) 4-inch flowers. These are triangular in form; the dorsal sepal is hooded and orange red, strongly veined with bright red. The lateral sepals are bright red, the petals and lip inconspicuous.

Difficult to grow, this orchid is exacting as to water, soil, and temperature. It needs cool temperatures and a freely draining, neutral to acid growing medium based on sand and peat. The water it receives must be free of mineral salts and neutral to acid in reaction. Some hobbyists have had success growing *Disa* in pure coarse sand using hydroponic techniques (see page 23).

DRACULA

As befits their name, these orchids often appear threatening—or at the very least bizarre. The conspicuous part of the flower is the triangle formed by the three sepals. The points trail out into long tails, the colors tend to be muted and mottled, and the texture may be warty or shaggy, with hairs. The ridiculous petals are tiny, looking somewhat like eyes peering out from the depth of the flower, and the inflated lip resembles the nose of a sinister clown.

These were once included in the genus *Masdevallia* and grow under its general conditions. However, despite their better tolerance of heat, the draculas are fussier, needing cool temperatures, shade, high humidity coupled with good air movement, and constant moisture without sogginess. They have no pseudobulbs; the stalked leaves arise directly from the rhizome. Draculas should be grown in a loose, open medium in slatted wood or wire baskets, so that the flowers can emerge from the sides or bottom. They are definitely not orchids for beginners to grow.

Dracula chimaera (Masdevallia chimaera). The leathery leaves are 10 inches long and 2 inches wide, the inflorescence up to 20 inches long. Flowers are roughly 6 inches wide, but each sepal ends in a 6-inch tail, bringing the overall measurement to 12 to 15 inches. The flower is buff colored and heavily spotted in maroon, with maroon tails. The entire flower is covered with hairs and warty growths. The flowering season is unpredictable.

D. erythrochaete. Less threatening in appearance than those of *D. chimaera,* the flowers of this species are an inch wide, with 2-inch tails terminating each sepal. The

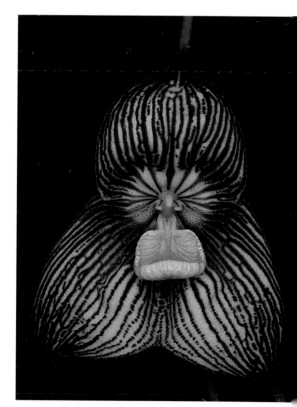

Dracula vampira 'Bela Lugosi' FCC/AOS

flower is creamy white, deepening to grayish or pinkish shades with maroon dots toward the center. Its tails are reddish brown. Blooms several times a year.

D. vampira. Drooping flower stalks carry flowers that may reach a foot across, colored yellowish white to yellowish green and striped along the length of the sepals in brownish black. And yes, Virginia, there is a selection named for Bela Lugosi.

EPIPACTIS

See "Hardy Orchids," pages 47–51.

GONGORA

Drooping inflorescences bearing fantastically shaped flowers characterize these orchids from the American tropics. The heavily ribbed pseudobulbs produce thin-textured, heavily veined leaves. Flowers are small, complex in structure, fragrant, and neatly and rather formally arranged on the hanging stems.

Grow them in intermediate to warm temperatures and light shade, in baskets or hanging pots filled with a loose, fast-draining medium. They thrive in high humidity and like frequent watering. When plants are in bud, rest them by withholding water for a brief period. Buyer beware: the names of the species are both confused and confusing.

Gongora armeniaca (G. cornuta). The 2-inch flowers are yellow to orange, sometimes spotted in red. Summer bloom.

G. galeata. The foot-long drooping inflorescence carries yellowish brown or rust-colored flowers with a hooked lip.

G. horichiana (G. armeniaca bicornuta). This plant's flowers are bright red.

G. quinquenervis. This variable species may include plants known as *G. bufonia* and *G. maculata.* Its drooping spikes may be 3 feet long and its flowers yellow, red, white, or greenish, with or without spots and stripes.

Gongora

GOODYERA

See "Hardy Orchids," pages 47–51.

LOCKHARTIA

The plants are clumps of unbranched erect or drooping stems sheathed by the broad bases of the short leaves. The general effect is that of a braided watch chain. The flowers are borne in clusters on short spikes and resemble those of oncidiums. They prefer bright light, a humid atmosphere, and intermediate temperatures. Grow these orchids in bark and water them freely, but withhold some water in winter. They flower over an extended period—sometimes all year.

Lockhartia lunifera. The stems are one foot tall and erect. The flower spike usually forms at the end of the stem and contains one or a few half-inch golden yellow flowers with a sprinkling of tiny purple dots.

L. oerstedtii. The erect stems are 1½ feet tall. The flowers appear singly or in twos. A little less than an inch wide, they are bright yellow with an elaborately shaped lip marked with brown swellings.

LUDISIA DISCOLOR (HAEMARIA DISCOLOR)

Grown for its foliage rather than its flowers, this is very likely the easiest orchid to grow. It thrives under the same conditions as an African violet—a rich, loose house plant potting mix, moderate light level, cool to warm temperatures, ample water with good drainage, and occasional light feeding. The stems branch and creep, rising at the ends to form rosettes of velvety, bronzy brown, 3-inch, broadly oval leaves veined with red. A slender flower spike 6 inches tall holds many tiny white flowers with yellow lips.

Easy to propagate, this is a good plant to share with friends: small pieces broken off root readily in moist potting mix. The plant is sometimes sold as *L. discolor dawsoniana* or *L. dawsoniana*.

LYCASTE

Lycaste plants are deciduous or semievergreen, dropping leaves in dry winters. Their leaves are large, thin in texture, and pleated. The flowers appear from the base of the pseudobulbs before the leaves expand, or just as they begin to expand. Each short stem carries a single flower, but the pseudobulbs may produce many of these flowering stems. The flowers consist of three large sepals and two smaller inner petals (usually of a contrasting color) that form a hood above or around the lip. Although the flowers are long lasting on the plant, they are easily bruised once cut.

Grow lycastes in light shade and cool to intermediate temperatures, using a cymbidium mix or a bark-based mix. The plants need little water during winter, but heavy watering should begin when the flowers and leaves appear and continue until new growth is completed. In addition to the species listed below, many other species and a number of hybrids and selections are occasionally available.

Lycaste aromatica. Each 6-inch flower stem carries a single 3-inch flower, but each pseudobulb may produce a dozen stems. The sepals are yellow with a greenish tinge, the petals bright yellow. Flowers are strongly cinnamon scented when they bloom, in late winter and spring.

L. brevispatha. Two-inch flowers on 4-inch stalks have pale green, pink-spotted sepals and white to rose petals. The lip is white.

L. campbellii. The flowers are small, with green sepals, yellow petals, and a deeper yellow lip.

L. cruenta. This species resembles *L. aromatica,* but has 4-inch flowers.

L. denningiana. Winter flowers droop on long (20-inch) stems; they are large (5 to 6 inches across), with pale green segments and a bright orange lip. Leaves remain on the plant from season to season. It appreciates cool, dry conditions.

L. deppei. Similar to *L. aromatica,* but sepals of the 4-inch flowers are green, heavily spotted with red; the petals are white, the lip yellow. Blooms in spring to fall.

TOP: *Lycaste cochleata*
BOTTOM: *Lycaste skinneri alba* 'Snow White' AM/AOS

L. macrobulbon. The 2½-inch flowers have greenish yellow sepals and whitish yellow petals. The lip is yellow with some brown spotting. The flowers bloom in spring and summer.

L. macrophylla. The 3½-inch flowers have green sepals with pinkish brown edges, white petals with pink spots, and a white lip with pink dots. Spring or summer bloom is usual, but this one may bloom at any time.

L. skinneri (L. virginalis). The leaves can reach 30 inches in length. The 12-inch flower stems bear 6-inch flowers, whose sepals are white to deep pink, their petals deeper pink to red, and their lips white to pale pink with deeper pink spots. There is a pure white variety, *L. s. alba,* and a number of named selections. This is the national flower of Guatemala. These plants do not require so decided a winter rest as other lycastes. Bloom is in fall and winter.

L. trifoliata. Small plants produce small, apple green flowers with a heavily fringed white lip.

MASDEVALLIA

Native to misty mountain forests, these small orchids need cool, humid conditions along with good air movement. Because the plants take up little room, enthusiasts in favored areas can amass large collections (one grower offers 40 species). They grow out-of-doors in light shade with little protection where frosts are rare and summer temperatures moderate, and they are easy to manage where low night temperatures can be guaranteed.

These plants have no pseudobulbs; stems bearing a single leaf arise in clumps from the creeping rhizome. The leaves are narrow, leathery, and dark green. Flowers arise singly or in few-flowered clusters from the joint between leaf and stem.

The basic shape of the flower is a short tube broadening out into a triangle composed of the three sepals. The sepals usually end in long tails, and the flowers are large for the size of the plant. Petals and lip are tiny, scarcely visible inside the flower tube.

The 350 or so species entice collectors with their bright colors and odd shapes. A fad among collectors at the end of the 19th century, they faded from view for decades but have lately made a strong comeback. A few (noted below) will tolerate intermediate to warm temperatures.

Grow masdevallias in small pots filled with a medium based on fine bark. Many growers have also had excellent results with sphagnum moss. They should never become dry, but soggy conditions at the root can kill them. Their small size and love of relatively low light makes them good subjects for growing under lights.

Masdevallia ayabacana. Clumps of 10-inch leaves give rise to 18-inch stems that produce a succession of large yellow flowers shaded rusty red. Tolerates warmth.

M. chimaera. See DRACULA CHIMAERA, page 101.

M. coccinea. Leaves extend to 9 inches; flower stalks up to 16 inches long carry a single 6-inch flower, usually red but sometimes purple, pink, or white. The upper sepal is all tail; the lower two resemble baggy "Dutch boy" trousers nipped in at the ankles.

Masdevallia strobelii 'J&L'

Masdevallia Proud Prince 'Royalty' AM/AOS

This species likes cool summers. The variety *harryana (M. c. harryana)* is blood red. Spring bloom.

M. floribunda. The small (to 4 inches) plant produces many small, bell-shaped, short-tailed flowers from sprawling or trailing stems. The flower color is yellow dotted with many crimson spots; it may vary to purple.

M. ignea (M. militaris). The leaves reach 8 inches in length, the flower stem, 16 inches. The latter produces a single 3½-inch, bright red to deep red flower with a drooping upper sepal. The plant blooms several times a year.

M. reichenbachiana. Clumps of 6-inch leaves produce somewhat taller stems carrying one to three 2½-inch flowers that are red on the outer portions, white within. Spring to autumn bloom. This species can take warm conditions.

M. rolfeana. Very like *M. reichenbachiana,* this differs in being a shorter plant with somewhat smaller, solid red flowers. Spring and summer bloom. Tolerates warmth.

M. strobelii. The 5-inch leaves are overtopped by a 6-inch flowering stem producing from one to four flowers in succession; these may repeat bloom for several years. The 1½-inch mildly fragrant flowers are white with a bright orange center and orange tails. Tolerates warmth.

M. tovarensis. Six-inch flower stalks bear one to four 1½-inch white flowers in succession, with repeat bloom in later years. Tolerates warmth.

M. veitchiana. The leaves are 10 inches tall, the flower stem 18 inches with a single 8-inch orange to vermilion flower that glistens with a profusion of tiny purple hairs. Early summer bloom.

MAXILLARIA

The plants are variable in habit, but those commonly grown greatly resemble *Lycaste,* with pseudobulbs bearing a single leaf and flowers arising singly from the bases of the pseudobulbs. The flowers also resemble those of *Lycaste.* the large sepals produce a three-cornered flower with smaller petals and lip in the center. Most thrive in warm or intermediate temperatures, and require considerable shade.

Maxillaria nigrescens. The pleated leaves are 1 foot long. Flower stalks 5 inches tall carry 5-inch spidery-looking flowers of dark red, with a nearly black lip. Winter bloom.

M. picta. The 5- to 8-inch flower stalks carry thick-textured 2½-inch tawny yellow flowers, heavily marked with purplish brown. Winter bloom.

M. sanderiana. The flowers are fragrant, 5 to 6 inches across, and ivory spotted with blood red. The white lip has yellow and red markings. Summer to fall bloom.

M. tenuifolia. This one is a pet because of its remarkable fragrance, which exactly mimics that of a freshly baked coconut pie. The leaves are grasslike, rising from tiny pseudobulbs strung along a rambling or climbing rhizome. Stems 2 inches long support 2-inch, thick, fleshy flowers of variable color—usually dark red marked with yellow. Summer to autumn bloom.

M. variabilis. This nearly everblooming species resembles *M. tenuifolia,* but the flower color ranges from pale yellow to dark red, and the flowers are less than an inch wide. They have a mild lemon scent in the morning.

Maxillaria tenuifolia

PHAIUS TANKERVILLEAE (P. GRANDIFOLIUS)

NUN'S ORCHID. Of the 50 or so species in this genus, only this one is likely to be seen. A large terrestrial orchid, it is native over a wide range from China to Australia, and plants from the northern regions can withstand temperatures down to 40°F (5°C), possibly lower. In fact, although in general the plants like warm to intermediate temperatures, they need a period of winter chilling to bloom satisfactorily. During that time they need little water. Pseudobulbs to 3 inches tall support two to four large (1- to 3-foot), heavily pleated evergreen leaves. Flower spikes to 4 feet tall arise from the base of the pseudobulbs and carry up to 20 fragrant, 4- to 5-inch brownish red flowers with a white lip. Bloom is in spring. Grow this orchid in a rich, loose, soil-based mix with a high organic content. In the deep South and Southern California, plants can grow outdoors. Elsewhere they can spend the summer outside in light shade.

Phaius tankervilleae 'Big Boy'

PLEIONE

These deciduous dwarf orchids have showy flowers and are quite hardy, being native to high mountains in India and China. They can be grown out-of-doors in light shade where frosts are rare and summer temperatures moderate, provided that they have perfect drainage, a rich peaty soil, and a minimal amount of protection in winter (meaning shelter from excessive rain and deep freezing). The small round or top-shaped pseudobulbs produce one or two thin, pleated leaves. Flowers are large for the size of the plant and resemble small cattleyas. In most species they appear just as the leaves begin to show. Repot plants each year before growth begins, using a rich, highly organic, well-drained soil mix. Set several close together in a shallow pot for a big show, burying only the bottom quarter of the bulb. Water to begin growth; flowers will appear in the spring, followed by foliage. Continue to water and feed well until foliage yellows; then gradually dry off.

Pleione formosana

Pleione bulbocodioides. Purple, 3-inch flowers on 6-inch stalks have a white lip marked with reddish spots.

P. formosana. The 3- to 4-inch flowers are purple (sometimes white or pink); the fringed lip has a yellow center with brownish red markings.

P. forrestii. The flowers are yellow with brownish red spots on the lip.

P. praecox. This species resembles *P. bulbocodioides,* but its flowers are borne one or two to the spike in autumn as the leaves turn yellow.

PLEUROTHALLIS

This is another huge genus containing over 1,000 species. Most are small (some tiny indeed) with small, unshowy flowers that are nevertheless interesting for the oddity of their form—especially as seen under a magnifying glass. Many have unusual foliage. The pleurothallids are an acquired taste, but many people collect them avidly.

These plants lack pseudobulbs; instead, the leaves emerge in clumps directly from the rhizome. In many species the flowering stem appears to emerge from the middle of

Pleurothallis marmorata

the leaf. What produces this impression is that the leaf stalk and midrib surround the flower stalk for most of its length. Give these orchids cool to intermediate temperatures and partial shade.

The species are so many, so diverse, and so widely misnamed that compiling a list is difficult. If you are interested, members of your local orchid society will share their knowledge—and likely their plants as well.

SOBRALIA

These large, showy terrestrial orchids somewhat resemble reeds or gingers *(Hedychium)* in growth habit, forming clumps of leafy stems. The flowers, which are formed like cattleyas, are borne at the top of those stems. The showy flowers are generally short-lived, but new ones appear over a long season.

Pot them in a mix appropriate for cymbidiums and water lavishly until the stems are fully grown; then reduce watering for a month. They prefer intermediate to warm temperatures and tolerate sun except when in bloom (during spring, summer, and early fall). These make impressive tub plants.

Sobralia macrantha
'Voodoo Priestess' AM/AOS

Sobralia leucoxantha. This 3-foot plant has 4- to 5-inch white flowers with yellow to orange markings in the center. Pure yellow forms also exist.

S. macrantha. A stately plant, this can grow to 7 feet—although 3 feet is more likely—and produces purplish red, 4- to 9-inch blossoms during spring and summer. Among its variants are plants with deep red or pure white flowers.

STANHOPEA

The stanhopeas are among the more bizarrely spectacular of orchids. The flowers are large, powerfully fragrant, fleshy, heavy, and short-lived (though produced in abundance). Give them cool to warm temperatures and partial shade. Water and feed them freely until the pseudobulbs have ripened; then reduce watering and increase the light supply.

Their form has been compared to giant moths, a sheep's skull, a flying bird with raised wings—even an eagle flying off with a squid! The complicated lip contains a scent-producing body to lure in the bee, a chute and bucket into which the bee falls, and an escape hatch that ensures that the bee will pick up some pollen on its way out.

Plant stanhopeas in a slatted wood or wire basket lined with sphagnum and filled with a coarse bark mix, with added leaf mold and dried cow manure. The pseudobulbs produce one (rarely two) large, broad, pleated leaves. The inflorescence grows downward, burrowing through its planting mix and emerging from the bottom of the basket.

Stanhopea oculata. The 4- to 6-inch flowers, three to six per inflorescence, are white to yellow and spotted with reddish purple, with two dark eyes on the lip. Summer bloom.

Stanhopea tigrina nigroviolacea 'Predator' FCC/AOS

S. tigrina. The 8-inch flowers, two to four per inflorescence, are yellow, barred and spotted with purplish brown. Summer to fall bloom.

S. wardii. Ten to twelve 6-inch flowers range in color from greenish white to deep yellow, with a fine sprinkling of red dots.

VANILLA PLANIFOLIA (V. FRAGRANS)

Of the many species only this, the vanilla of commerce, is likely to be seen — and then only in a sizable greenhouse (though it will grow and bloom indoors). A climbing vine that theoretically can grow to any length, it needs room, warm surroundings, bright light, and plenty of water throughout the year. Start the plant in a pot beneath a vertical piece of tree fern or a pole wrapped in sphagnum. As the plant elongates, support it with ties to the greenhouse framework. Don't fret if the stem dies off at ground level; aerial roots will keep the vine growing. The stems are thin, the 6-inch leaves thick and fleshy, and the short-lived, 5-inch flowers yellowish green. Hand pollination will induce the plant to produce vanilla beans.

ZYGOPETALUM

Zygopetalum

Two species and many hybrids and named selections of *Zygopetalum* are becoming popular, especially in coastal California and similar climates. There they can be grown like cymbidiums, enjoying the same planting mix, light conditions, and watering and feeding regime. They like cool to intermediate temperatures, but are slightly more sensitive to cold than are cymbidiums.

The tightly clustered pseudobulbs are sheathed by the bases of the evergreen, strap-shaped leaves growing in opposite ranks like a fan. Flower spikes rise from the base of the newest pseudobulb. The large, very fragrant flowers are usually a tiger-striped blend of green and maroon; the lips are white, finely netted with bluish violet to solid dark purple. Both of the species listed here are fall to winter blooming.

Zygopetalum
Blue Banks 'Baywood' HCC/AOS

Zygopetalum intermedium. The inflorescence reaches 16 inches and has a half dozen or more 3-inch flowers.

Z. mackayi. The inflorescence is taller (to 28 inches) than that of *Z. intermedium.* One should not be too dogmatic about the difference, however; many experts feel that most of the plants sold are actually *Z. intermedium.*

Many fine named selections and hybrids exist, among them *Z.* Warringal Wonder and *Z.* B. G. White 'Stonehurst', a heat-tolerant variety that thrives and blooms everywhere.

GLOSSARY

In this book you will find comparatively few technical terms. Words like spike, umbel, thyrse, and raceme are meaningful to botanists, but to only a few gardeners. For instance, most orchid fanciers refer to any orchid inflorescence as a spike. Technically, however, a spike is an unbranched inflorescence in which the flowers are borne directly on one common stalk. In this book we use the word to mean an actual spike as the botanist understands it. To cover the multiplicity of floral arrangements found among orchids we most often use the term inflorescence, which means either the disposition of flowers on a plant or the flowering portion of a plant.

aerial roots. Roots that arise above ground, from either the stem or the base of the plant.

alliance. A tribe, or group of related genera. Among orchids, many of these genera can crossbreed with other genera.

alternate. Describes leaves or flowers that are disposed along a stem or branch in twos, but on different sides and at different heights. There is only one leaf or inflorescence at each node on the stem. Compare with **opposite.**

anther. The portion of a flower that bears pollen.

anther cap. In orchids, a cap of tissue that covers the clusters of pollen.

arching. Curving gently outward and downward.

axil. The angle between a branch or stem and any organ (bud, flower, or shoot) extending from it.

back bulb. A pseudobulb that has completed its growth cycle and become dormant. It serves as a storage organ and may bear a dormant bud. Under favorable conditions, this bud may develop into a new plant if the pseudobulb is severed from the parent.

basal. Arising from the base of a plant, from either the rhizome or a short or buried stem.

bifoliate. Having two leaves at the top of the pseudobulb (describes one type of cattleya). Compare with **unifoliate.**

bisexual. Flowers that have both male organs (stamens) and female organs (pistils). Such flowers are also called perfect.

botanicals. *See* **species.**

bract. A leaflike organ (actually, a modified leaf) that serves to protect a flower, bud, or shoot.

cane. A long, narrow pseudobulb, usually having many joints, or nodes.

clone. Any asexually propagated (by division, cutting, or tissue culture) offspring of a single parent plant. A clone is identical to its parent. Among orchids, such a plant is likely to be a choice selection.

column. A single fleshy organ at the center of the flower, containing both stamens and pistil. The organ is unique to orchids.

deciduous. Not evergreen; shedding leaves that are no longer functioning—either once a year or as a response to some climatic event.

dorsal. In orchid talk, used principally to denote the uppermost sepal of a flower. Compare with **lateral.**

epiphyte. A plant that grows on another plant but does not depend on its host for nourishment, as a parasite does.

evergreen. Possessing foliage that persists for at least one year, or through one complete cycle of plant growth.

Miltonia Rainbow Falls 'Terry' HCC/AOS

Continued on page 110>

grex. From the Latin for flock; a name given to all the offspring of a cross between two species. No matter how often the cross is repeated, even with different individual plants representing the species, the offspring are considered to be the same grex. The name is printed in roman type with an initial capital letter, as in *Phragmipedium* × Grande. Any selected plant from this grex that is propagated by division or meristem culture will have its name enclosed in single quotation marks; for example, *Phragmipedium* × Grande 'The Wizard'. *See also* **hybrid.**

heterosis. Hybrid vigor, or the increased strength and the tolerance of varying conditions that are often found in the offspring of different species or genera.

hooded. Describes a flower part arched over or partially enclosed by another flower part.

hybrid. A plant that is the offspring of two different species or genera. *See also* **grex.**

hydroponics. Literally, "water work": a technique of growing plants in a sterile medium (or no medium at all) and flooding the roots periodically with a nutrient solution.

internode. That portion of a stem, cane, or pseudobulb located between two nodes, or joints.

keiki. A plantlet that develops high up on a cane, pseudobulb, or flower stem. When it has developed a sufficient root system, it may be detached and grown separately.

labellum. The lip, or third petal of the orchid flower, which has been modified in shape and color to lure a pollenizing insect.

Cattleya walkeriana alba

lateral. Pertaining to the side; on orchids, the lateral sepals are the lower pair of sepals. Compare with **dorsal.**

lead. The growing point of a sympodial orchid (such as a cattleya). Its lower portion lengthens the rhizome and develops roots. The upper portion becomes a pseudobulb and eventually produces leaves and flowers. A large plant may have several leads clustered along one side, called the leading edge.

lip. *See* **labellum.**

lithophyte. A plant that grows on rocks; many orchids do so, taking nourishment from mosses, litter, rain, and their own dead tissue.

mericlone. A plant propagated by tissue culture from meristematic tissue. *See* **meristem** and **clone.**

meristem. Undifferentiated tissue that is capable of developing into specialized tissue such as root, leaf, or stem. Also, in orchid talk, a plant produced by culturing meristematic tissue.

monopodial. Describes a type of plant growth in which new tissue is produced indefinitely from the tip of the plant. Branching is absent or little developed. Phalaenopsis and palms are good examples. Compare with **sympodial.**

multigeneric. Having more than two genera in the ancestry.

mycorrhiza. Fungi associated with, and beneficial to, the roots of a plant. In orchid propagation, mycorrhiza were essential to the germination of seeds before sterile nutrient growth media were devised. They may also be essential to the survival of some terrestrial orchids.

node. A joint, or point on a stem at which leaves, flowers, or other organs arise or have the potential to arise.

opposite. Describes leaves disposed along a stem or branch in twos, at the same height but on opposing sides. There are two leaves or inflorescences at each node on the stem. Compare with **alternate.**

petal. One of the inner whorl of organs surrounding the sexual parts of the flower. They are often colorful and attractive to pollenizing insects. Compare with **sepal.**

pleated. Folded lengthwise, as in a fan.

pseudobulb. A thickened, bulbous stem that arises from the rhizome and serves as a water and nutrient storage organ.

raft. A structure formed of wooden slats, used to support orchids that need especially fast drainage and constant root aeration.

Brassia verrucosa

rhizome. A stem that produces roots and above-ground organs such as stems, pseudobulbs, and flowers. In epiphytic orchids it is usually found on the surface; in terrestrial orchids it may be underground. The rhizome may be long, or so short as to be unnoticeable.

sepal. One of the outer whorl of organs surrounding the sexual parts of the flower. In some orchids (notably *Masdevallia*), the sepals join together to form a tube containing the other flower parts. Compare with **petal.**

sheath. A tubular structure surrounding some plant part. In orchids (notably in cattleyas), a leaflike structure containing the developing inflorescence at the end of the pseudobulb.

species. A group of plants sharing common attributes and occurring in nature (as opposed to the hybrids bred by human hands). Also, in orchid talk, one of the less-often-grown orchids (compared with the mass-produced hybrids). In the latter sense it is also frequently called a botanical.

spur. A tubular downward and outward extension of a flower that secretes nectar.

sympodial. Describes a type of plant growth in which branching occurs when the terminal bud flowers or dies; subsequent growth proceeds from side buds. Cattleyas and bearded iris are good examples. Compare with **monopodial.**

synsepalum. An organ resulting from the fusion of the two lower sepals of a slipper orchid. It is found below and behind the lip, or pouch.

terete. Cylindrical, pencil-shaped; used to describe a type of leaf or stem.

terrestrial. Growing in the soil.

tessellated. Describes leaves marked with small checkerboard squares, giving them a mottled effect.

tuber. A swollen, usually underground, plant organ (stem, branch, or root) used for food storage. Many terrestrial orchids grow from tubers.

unifoliate. Having a single leaf per pseudobulb (used to describe one kind of cattleya). Compare with **bifoliate.**

velamen. The corky outer layer of epiphytic orchid roots, whose function is to absorb atmospheric moisture.

whorl. Three or more leaves, flowers, or branches arranged in a circle at one point around the main stem.

Epidendrum pseudepidendrum

INDEX

Page numbers in **boldface type** indicate main entries in an encyclopedia section; those in *italic type* indicate photographs.